The Phoenicians

A Captivating Guide to the History of Phoenicia and the Impact Made by One of the Greatest Trading Civilizations of the Ancient World

Free Bonus from Captivating History (Available for a Limited time)

Hi History Lovers!

Now you have a chance to join our exclusive history list so you can get your first history ebook for free as well as discounts and a potential to get more history books for free! Simply visit the link below to join.

Captivatinghistory.com/ebook

Also, make sure to follow us on Facebook, Twitter and Youtube by searching for Captivating History.

Contents

Introduction – Who Were the Phoenicians?

The Phoenicians remain one of the most enigmatic ancient civilizations, with historians and scholars prone to speculation and educated guesses. Although many Greek, Roman, and Egyptian writers reference the Phoenicians in trade records, military battles, and artistic transactions, few records were left by the original Phoenicians themselves, leaving modern scholars to fill in the blanks through educated guesses and material culture.

The ancient perception about this civilization was mixed. For every writer like Pomponius Mela who lavished praise upon the Phoenicians, there was another who derided the people as nothing more than cheats and hucksters who kept other states' trade stymied through stranglehold networks and ridiculous deals. Mela described them as such: "The Phoenicians were a clever race, who prospered in war and peace. They excelled in writing and literature, and in other arts, in seamanship, and in ruling an empire."[1]

[1] Pomponius Mela 1.12.

To dissect Mela's quote, the Phoenicians were great writers, yet they left almost no documents. They may have been excellent sailors and naval commanders, yet they built no territorial empire. They were stellar artists, yet their work contains few original elements. They may have been clever builders, yet their monuments crumbled. And the Phoenicians were a single civilization, yet they were split into city-states.

How could a civilization exist with so many contradictions, and how can modern historians utilize evidence that no longer seems to exist to uncover the truth?

Who were the enigmatic Phoenicians, why did their civilization crumble, and why should a modern audience care?

Read on to find out.

Chapter 1 – Origins

The origin of the Phoenician civilization had long been a mystery to those who were not members of it because of the secrecy with which the famous traders conducted themselves. Herodotus, a famous Greek historian, once wrote around 440 BCE that the Phoenicians were a people who left the shores of the Erythraean Sea and chose to settle around the Mediterranean.[2] From there, they plied their wares amongst the indigenous populations, creating one of the greatest trading civilizations in history.

Herodotus and many other Greeks thus believed the Phoenicians originated near the Erythraean Sea, which was a designation for the northwest Indian Ocean around the Gulf of Aden. This would have meant the Phoenicians came from Yemen or Somalia, although Herodotus later claimed Bahrain.[3] Another Greek historian, Strabo, would reiterate the belief that the Phoenicians hailed from Bahrain. However, archaeologists have discovered little evidence of any sort of large-scale human occupation of the region around the time the migration should have taken place: 2200 BCE to 1600 BCE. Instead, most of the city-states were based around contemporary Lebanon,

[2] Dates are referred to using the standard historic system of Before Common Era (BCE) and Common Era (CE).
[3] In contemporary times, Bahrain is an island nation in the Persian Gulf.

which is above modern Israel on the eastern coast of the Mediterranean Sea.

The people of the city of Tyre in South Lebanon maintain attachments to the Phoenicians, frequently noting the similarities between the names “Tylos,” an ancient name of Bahrain, and “Tyre.” They also point to similarities between the Persian Gulf and the culture of the Phoenicians. These claims actually have some scientific backing, as genetic studies have led some scientists to conclude that there is strong evidence that the Phoenicians were ethnically from Lebanon. The best of this evidence can be found in detailed genetic studies designed to examine the DNA fragments that exist in ancient skeletons.

Genetic Studies

Scientists have come a long way in the field of genetics, and they often work together with experts in the humanities to solve long unanswered questions about ancient peoples. Using DNA pulled directly from skeletons, geneticists and others can determine information about civilizations like the Phoenicians such as their heredity, nutrition, diet, and health. In 2008, a study published by Pierre Zalloua and his team of scientists revealed a possible connection between the Phoenicians and contemporary male populations in Lebanon and other regions in the Levant.

There were also distinct similarities between ancient Phoenician DNA and the samples taken from native individuals of southern Turkey, Malta, Sicily, Morocco, Spain, Sardinia, Ibiza, and Tunisia. These results resulted in the team concluding that the Phoenicians most likely hailed from Lebanon because they possessed a distinct genetic signature called haplogroup J2. The presence of similarities in other regions was deemed indicative of Phoenician expansion across the Mediterranean Sea following the rise of its civilization.[4]

---

[4]Pierre A. Zalloua, Daniel E. Platt, Mirvat El Sibai, Jade Khalife, et al. “Identifying Genetic Traces of Historical Expansions: Phoenician Footprints in the Mediterranean.”

In 2013, Zalloua led another study, this time testing more geographical communities to determine whether or not certain groups possessed a higher rate of what was termed the "Phoenician signature," or a distinct DNA sequence and genes that appeared to originate in the Phoenician civilization. Some communities did, in fact, have a higher rate of the Phoenician signature appearing in indigenous populations, which led Zalloua and his colleagues to conclude that Lebanon, the originating location of the Phoenicians, already possessed a diverse population consisting of "well-differentiated communities with their own genetic peculiarities" upon which religious and cultural divisions were then painted over.[5] In short, the Phoenicians did not represent a homogenous population of Lebanon but rather a particular ethnic group that rose to prominence and eventually unified the region, allowing the Phoenician signature to spread to new regions.

Other studies over the last two decades produced similar results but also identified the potential closest surviving relatives of the ancient Phoenicians by identifying genetic similarities. The closest contemporary ethnic group to the Phoenicians is the Levantine Semites, a category that includes a broad spectrum of Lebanese, Jewish, Palestinian, and Syrian individuals. There is also notable genetic similarity—sometimes as much as ninety percent—between the modern Lebanese population and the Bronze Age Sidonians.[6] [7] The Sidonians were Phoenicians from the city-state of Sidon, which was north of Tyre. They were famous glass producers.

However, finding out such information, while it reveals fascinating details about genetics and the movement of people, says little about

---

5 [43]

6 Lucotte, Gérard; Mercier, Géraldine (2003). "Y-chromosome DNA haplotypes in Jews: comparisons with Lebanese and Palestinians." *Genetic Testing.* **7** (1): 67–71. doi:10.1089/109065703321560976

7 Haber, Marc; Doumet-Serhal, Claude; Scheib, Christiana; Xue, Yali; Danecek, Petr; Mezzavilla, Massimo; Youhanna, Sonia; Martiniano, Rui; Prado-Martinez, Javier (2017-08-03). "Continuity and Admixture in the Last Five Millennia of Levantine History from Ancient Canaanite and Present-Day Lebanese Genome Sequences." *The American Journal of Human Genetics.* 101 (2): 274–282. doi:10.1016/j.ajhg.2017.06.013

the Phoenicians as a culture. To find this information and to understand the origins of the once-great trading civilization, one has to look at who the Phoenicians were as a society. And what they were was Canaanites.

A Cultural Ancestor

Wherever the Phoenicians may have come from, they were ultimately an offshoot of the Canaanites. Although most associate the Canaanites with the state of Canaan, the term actually refers to a series of indigenous peoples and populations that lived in an area in the ancient Near East called the Levant. The Levant is an approximate historical, geographical term used to refer to a large segment of the Eastern Mediterranean. It primarily includes what modern audiences call Lebanon, Syria, Jordan, Israel, and Palestine.

The Canaanites were Semitic-speaking peoples with a unique culture derived from ancient Mesopotamian traditions and religious practices. There were many different groups that could be considered Canaanites while still maintaining their own ethnical and cultural differences. One archaeologist, Jonathan N. Tubb, said it best when he stated the "Ammonites, Moabites, Israelites, and Phoenicians undoubtedly achieved their own cultural identities, and yet ethnically they were all Canaanites."[8] To be a Canaanite was not to be part of a monolith; it meant forging one's unique identity while sharing some cultural similarities with the other Semitic-speaking groups of the Levant.

As a unit, the Canaanites were forced to carve a unique niche for themselves in the ancient world because they lived in an arid region surrounded by powerful enemies like the Egyptians, Assyrians, Babylonians, Akkadians, and even Minoans from Crete. Creating a homeland was difficult, and a stable military was hard to feed and shelter while on the move. Eventually, the Canaanites discovered they operated well as intermediaries between other civilizations and

[8] Tubb, Johnathan N. (1998). *Canaanites. British Museum People of the Past.*

became traders, shuffling goods from one place to another and profiting handsomely.

One can see where the Phoenicians developed their unique flavor by watching how the Canaanites as a whole flocked to the coast and began to educate themselves about their neighbors and what powerful rulers desired. Over time, the Phoenicians would distinguish themselves from the Canaanites in a manner similar to the Israelites. The people, while originally Canaanites, developed their own distinct culture and identity, forming a new civilization in the process.

Maintaining power would always be a struggle. The Canaanites were plagued by climate changes and issues like drought and famine that made trade and feeding a population difficult. For thousands of years, the people were on the move, attempting to find a place where they could support themselves. They were around during the infamous Bronze Age Collapse, which was when many of the powerful civilizations of the Bronze Age—the period in human history where cultures discovered how to make bronze weapons and tools—suddenly hit a dark era. During the Bronze Age Collapse, civilizations starved and warred with one another potentially due to climate change and the arrival of a foreign enemy known only as the Sea Peoples.

But what did it mean for the Phoenicians to be Canaanites?

As Canaanites, the Phoenicians inherited a rich culture rooted in the traditions of Mesopotamia. The civilization spoke a Semitic language, or a variation of the Afroasiatic language family originating in the Middle East shared by many other civilizations. A contemporary example of a Semitic language would be Arabic, which originated in the same region and evolved over time from old Semitic tongues to what it is today. This gave the Phoenicians some cultural similarities with their neighbors while ensuring they stood apart from trading partners like the Greeks and Egyptians.

The Phoenicians would also inherit the Mesopotamian religion, which was polytheistic and rooted in tribalism and multiple cultures. They believed in a supreme god who had managed to produce lesser deities, and they often performed religious rites and rituals meant to boost agriculture, wealth, and health. They had a priesthood and a mythology that they shared with their other Canaanite neighbors, including the Israelites. Each region tended to worship a different god above all others, adding new complexities to the mix.

Finally, the Phoenicians inherited Canaanite social norms. This meant they tended to dress modestly, had extreme gender roles for men and women, built their homes using traditional methods, and molded their society around city-states filled with powerful nobles. Although the Canaanites have a bad reputation among many followers of Abrahamic religions because of their depiction in holy books, they were actually a complicated culture centered on trying to survive in a harsh world. The Phoenicians would carry this legacy as they carved for themselves a powerful reputation in the ancient world as the best and most cunning traders history has ever seen.

Chapter 2 – The World of the Phoenicians

In order to understand the massive trade network and interstate relationships cultivated by this unique civilization, readers need to understand just what constituted the world at this time. Although many ancient peoples knew of something greater than themselves, it is likely that none could comprehend the sheer enormity of the planet. Instead, their world consisted of the Mediterranean Sea, parts of Southern Europe, Northern Africa, and Western Asia. The Phoenicians went to key locations on each of these continents and established cities from which to trade, forming a small yet expansive state.

The Phoenicians started their civilization in a fertile and developed region known as the Levant. The Levant was one of the original cradles of civilization and included most of what contemporaries now consider the Middle East. The Phoenicians were based right along the Mediterranean coast, but they also had territory that expanded throughout modern Lebanon. This land was excellent for farming and included great cedar forests that supplied lumber for homes and ships.

The central Phoenician territory existed in an enviable position and thus came under attack regularly from neighboring states. The territory encompassed several notable passageways used for trading between Asia and Africa. Conquerors, kings, and warlords all wanted to control the region because it would mean untold wealth and numerous political advantages when attempting to subjugate rivals.

Although Phoenicia became well known for its navy, its people still needed to be protected from ground-based attacks. Over time, a strong military and sturdy city fortifications were developed in each individual settlement. The armies of the city-states would often work together but were still separate entities under the control of a variety of local generals. Even though the military never reached the heights of more powerful Mediterranean civilizations, the Phoenicians did have an advantage, as they were a nascent civilization that didn't emerge until the end of the Bronze Age, allowing them to transition their culture and society easier than other established civilizations into the Iron Age.

The Iron Age of the ancient Near East began around 1300 BCE, and it refers to the period of time when humans learned how to create and use iron to make implements, tools, and weapons. The Phoenicians first emerged as a distinct culture once the other civilizations in the Levant experienced a societal collapse that eliminated the majority of state power and left territories that were basically free pickings for anyone who could handle the numerous raiders and the mysterious Sea Peoples that had decimated more powerful civilizations.

Having emerged just before the Iron Age, the Phoenicians inherited much of the technology and social developments of their predecessors, including the Canaanites. They were able to use these elements in combination with the relative weakness of formally powerful enemies like Egypt to carve an advantageous position along the coast, from which they could control commerce from heavily fortified city-states.

However, the Phoenicians would be unable to form their monopoly on trade until after the Bronze Age Collapse and thus dealt with numerous other powerful civilizations in the region that posed imminent threats to the safety and success of Phoenician civilization. These were the juggernauts of the ancient Levant, powerful groups that were advantageous and yet dangerous for the Phoenicians because of their proximity. The most important were the Assyrians, Greeks, Egyptians, Babylonians, and Persians, who would appear at different times throughout the lifespan of the Phoenician civilization.

Influential City-States

Because the Phoenicians were so spread out, they possessed numerous city-states that formed essential parts of their intricate maritime trade networks. All told, archaeologists have discovered around eighty separate city-states scattered through a diverse region. The most significant city-states were in the region of Lebanon, where the Phoenicians originated. Other influential settlements could be found in Algeria, Cyprus, Italy, Libya, Malta, Spain, Tunisia, Turkey, and Morocco. Historians also think the Phoenicians controlled certain ports in Portugal and Greece, including Lisbon.

Tyre

Tyre was an island city-state based off of the coast of Lebanon. It was constructed by rulers who used dirt, sand, and rocks from the nearby beaches to fill the space between two reefs, creating a spot on which the city could be built. Over time, rulers continued to enlarge and expand the territory, creating what should have been one of the most defensible locations in the Mediterranean. Unfortunately, the arrogance of the Tyrian monarchy led to the city being sacked by Alexander the Great in the 4th century BCE, resulting in most of the city being lost.

Tyre was influential as a port for commerce and trade, but it relied heavily on the mainland to keep it supplied with building materials, food, and fresh water. Ships traveled from the island to the coast to gather natural resources, and the city controlled nearby arable land for farming and livestock. Within the walls of Tyre, the locals gathered rainwater in cisterns and engaged in a variety of influential crafts, including dye-making, pottery production, and jewelry manufacturing.

Byblos

Byblos was a seaport and a significant city at the base of the Lebanese mountains that specialized in the creation and export of papyrus scrolls. The location was originally settled in the Neolithic period and was one of the oldest and most enduring Phoenician cities. It was conquered and turned into a vassal state by invaders multiple times throughout its history, but it served as the central jewel in the Phoenician crown of commerce for many centuries during the Phoenician golden age. There was plenty of access to fresh water and copper, making this a resource-rich urban center full of craftsmen and women who benefited from the labor of nearby farmers and shepherds.

Sidon

Sidon was another city-state located in modern-day Lebanon that served as an influential seaport for commerce and trade. It had been occupied since the Neolithic period and stood out from other urban centers by having access to lush cedar wood forests, hinterlands, and fertile agricultural territory. Dye-making was a popular activity because the city was near a cove where divers could locate murex snails, which were necessary for making a luxurious and unique purple dye. In contemporary times, Sidon is well known in archaeological circles for having some of the most preserved tombs and burial grounds, providing much-needed insight into the rituals of the Phoenicians and their view on the afterlife.

Carthage

Carthage is one of the city-states many have heard about because of its famous rivalry with Rome, but it began as a colony of Tyre in North Africa (in modern-day Tunisia) that eventually rose to become a powerful city-state. Carthage was heavily militaristic, supplying the Phoenicians with weapons and formidable war elephants. However, the people also made pottery, developed their own writing style and language, and produced massive amounts of text that would be burned when Rome sacked the city.

Besides these four major players, there were dozens of additional cities and colonies that formed the massive Phoenician trade network. Most of the evidence about their comings and goings comes from archaeological excavations, which are able to locate the skeletons of temples and other significant buildings, as well as distinctly Phoenician artifacts. These other locations include:

- Beirut
- Tripoli
- Sarepta
- Baalbek
- Hippo
- Icosium
- Marion
- Tharros
- Leptis Magna
- Callista
- Utica
- Lisbon
- Sexi

Some of these names will no doubt sound familiar to contemporary readers. These territories were spread out over a broad area and encompassed locations like North Africa, Cyprus, Sicily, the Iberian Peninsula, modern-day Turkey, modern-day Algeria, and modern-day Lebanon.

Chapter 3 – Political and Legal Structures

The first step in understanding the complexities of a civilization with little-known history is to take a look at what scholars do know. What they do have an understanding of is how the Phoenicians conducted their daily lives and operated their city-states. One of the underlying fundamentals of civilization is the political state, an entity that many ancient historians believe separated humans from their hunter-gatherer roots and helped develop a society based on agriculture.

The Phoenician civilization did not consist of a single state but rather several significant powers that organized themselves into hotspots of influence and trade. These would be known as the city-states, or political entities that controlled a major city and much of the surrounding territory around it. Another similar example of this type of civilization would be the ancient Greeks, who operated from individual settlements that controlled nearby agricultural lands.

The Political Structure: Social Classes Abound

The political structure of the Phoenician civilization varied by location and adopted the customs of neighbors and trading partners alike. Throughout much of the culture's history, Phoenicia was split between several independent city-states that shared a similar culture but kept political power divided between a series of hereditary monarchies. The most famous of these city-states were notable trading ports like Tyre, Sidon, and Byblos. Phoenicia never became a single political entity, and the kings would exercise almost complete control until the destruction of the civilization.

Before annihilation, though, political power was split due to the presence of multiple social classes and influential families. While the monarchs were the head of each city-state, they relied upon an administration to carry out the actual governance of the territory. In most cases, the administrators of the government were members of a class of priests as well as significant noble households. The nobles could provide resources like food and soldiers, meaning it was important for the monarchs to remain on their good sides. While almost all noble families were born into their position, some individuals managed to join this elite rank by making a fortune in international trade.

Because the city-states were independent of one another but shared a similar culture, they cooperated to foster a powerful empire built on trade. Many historians compare the Phoenicians to the ancient Greeks, who lived in city-states like Athens and Sparta, shared a culture, and occasionally got along to defend against external enemies. While the Phoenicians would sometimes unite their armies, the city-states emphasized cooperation not so much for defense but instead to build an economic powerhouse in the Levant and the nearby Mediterranean Sea.

Separate city-states would be the most powerful at different times in history. The city-state with the most resources thus had more political influence and power compared to the others. This meant the political structure of Phoenicia was liable to change based on which region was the wealthiest or possessed the most soldiers. For example, Sidon was the most powerful city-state between the 12th and 11th centuries BCE and, therefore, was able to bully or coerce the nearby city-states of Tyre and Byblos into doing what it wanted. In the 10th century BCE, Tyre became the most powerful. Although the Phoenician city-states avoided making formal alliances, they were not above making informal agreements structured around force and the ever-present trade.

When it came to foreign policy, the city-states were on their own. Phoenicia had no single recognized ruler or council, so places like Sidon and Tyre could choose to help whichever allies they wanted. If the monarch of one wished to assist the Greeks, for example, he could. If he did not, there was no political power pressuring him into joining a war effort. This could be seen throughout the history of Phoenicia. The best example is during the famous war between Greece and Persia when each city-state in Phoenicia gradually chose to help Xerxes by sending ships to bolster the Persian emperor's navy. This was not a cohesive decision but one born out of convenience and a desire for power. After all, Persia controlled several of the Phoenician territories by this point in history, and the remaining independent city-states did not want to incur the ire and wrath of Xerxes.

Hereditary Monarchies

Members of the hereditary monarchies are the most well-known Phoenician political figures. Although they did not commemorate their achievements through sculptures or artwork like the pharaohs of Egypt or the kings of Greece, Phoenician rulers did leave their names on tomb inscriptions. Archaeologists have been able to date coffins and temples, and historians have discovered numerous references to the Phoenician kings in surviving primary sources.

According to tomb inscriptions, the hereditary monarchs managed to wield absolute power until the 7th century BCE when discontent members of Phoenician society decided they would like a better slice of the political power pie. At the same time, it is obvious that the monarchs could not tax their populations much due to the small size of the civilization. Instead, kings needed to trade and fund expeditions to acquire rare goods and make money by taxing merchants.

When talking about the monarchs, it's important to note that women, while they could become queens, did not rule on their own. They were not as important as the male heirs and rarely had their names inscribed in the annals of history. The right to rule was passed down from father to son. If there were no male heirs, the husband of the closest female heir would become the new king. Historians have created a somewhat comprehensive list of the different monarchs of city-states like Sidon and Tyre. Savvy readers will realize that not a single name belongs to a woman and that many rulers incorporated "baal" in their names. In early Phoenician history, Ba'al was the chief deity and viewed as the supreme lord of the cosmos. Referencing him in royal naming practices was seen as a form of legitimizing the monarchy.

In Byblos, the line of succession looked like this:

- c. 1000 BCE Ahiram
- 980 BCE Ittobaal
- 940 BCE Abibaal
- 920 BCE Yehimilk
- 900 BCE Elibaal
- 880 BCE Shipitbaal

The annals of Tyre and other complementary sources produce the following list of reigning kings for Tyre:

- 969-936 BCE Hiram I
- 935-919 BCE Baal-Eser I
- 918-910 BCE Abdastrato
- 909-898 BCE Methustratos
- 897-889 BCE Astharymos
- 888 BCE Phelles
- 887-856 BCE Ithobaal I

- 855-830 BCE Baal-Eser II
- 829-821 BCE Mattan II
- 820-774 BCE Pygmalion
- 750-740 BCE Ithobaal II
- 739-730 BCE Hiram II
- 730-729 BCE Mattan II
- 729-694 BCE Elulaios
- 680-640 BCE Baal I
- 591-573 BCE Ithobaal III
- Baal II
- Mattan III
- Hiram III

The monarchs possessed reasonably long reigns for ancient history, with most having power for two to three decades. Only one inscription from Sidon is a woman, Unmiashtart, who became a regent for her son in the 5th century BCE. The only other influential female political figure comes from a quasi-mythological source and is Dido, the famous sister of Pygmalion. She was said to have left Tyre along with like-minded nobles and helped establish the city of Carthage on the northern coast of Africa.

The Priesthood

The priesthood was considered a separate class from the nobility, although most of the members came from the royal line, as well as leading merchant families. Priests were responsible for the maintenance of significant temples as well as the performance of rituals intended to maintain Phoenician society and please the gods. In multiple cases, records indicate that priests could also become royals or were closely entwined with the family. One famous example is Ozbaal, who became the king of Byblos but who was the son of a priest of Baalat named Paltibaal.

Priests worked closely with the monarchs of the city-states because, in Phoenician culture, the office of king carried religious rights and obligations. The king was seen as a representative of the gods and worked to ensure they were seen as just and righteous, as well as powerful. Occasionally, a king might claim to actually be a god incarnate on earth, although this maneuver was opposed by the priests. To become a priest, a man needed to be born in a noble family and undergo years of training. Priests had access to places commoners and even other nobles could not go, particularly the inner sanctums of many of the temples.

Senior Officials

If a man wanted power in Phoenician society, he could become a senior official to the king. Like priests, senior officials could only be nobles and needed to be elders. The king of city-states like Tyre would consult with elders for advice about the best course of political action. According to an ancient Greek historian named Arrian, the Phoenician senior officials would be called upon to make important decisions when the king was indisposed. Other historians from nearby trading partners also mentioned the council and believed it held the most power in the city-states. Membership no doubt only belonged to senior nobles and influential merchants, and it is unknown whether the king had to bow to their will. There is some evidence, though, that the council could force the king to adhere to their decisions in times of crisis.

Besides the council, the other two positions of importance were the governor and the commander of the army. Each city-state would have one each, and their roles focused on administration, tax collection, and coordinating the defense of the city. The governor also needed to supervise the courts and ensure justice was served. Unfortunately, many details about these jobs are lacking because the texts taken from El Amarna, Cyprus, and Ugarit are fragmented.

Alternative Forms of Government

At some point, Tyre bucked the original monarchy and embraced a system of government in the 6th century BCE, where everything was controlled by a pair of judges called the *suffetes*. These judges were chosen from the most powerful noble families and appeared to exert almost dictator-like control over justice and the governance of the territory. This system would be adopted by Carthage later on.

Besides the *suffetes*, the kings of the Phoenician cities would also have to rule alongside an Assyrian governor when the Assyrians dominated the region in the 7th century BCE. Even official correspondence could not be opened without the governor present, and the king became more of a figurehead in a vassal state. This system would continue when the Babylonians arrived and Nebuchadnezzar II decided a minister needed to rule alongside the king of Tyre, a system continued by the Persians later on.

However, such systems tended to occur under imperialism and the vassalage of more powerful civilizations and were confined to captured city-states. Tyre perhaps experienced the most changes in government because it was captured again and again due to its desirable position on the coast of modern-day Lebanon.

Law and Order

Scholars possess little information about the administration of law and order by the Phoenicians. It is clear that they had a system of courts with judges and justices that were responsible for meting out punishments and solving disputes between citizens. Laws were also applied differently to the varying social classes, as the murder of a commoner by a noble was not punished as harshly as a regular man would be if he hurt or killed someone of the upper classes. Likewise, women possessed far fewer rights than their male counterparts, and slaves had almost no protections for themselves.

Because the Phoenicians were Canaanites culturally, they shared some similarities to the justice systems practiced by the Canaanites, Israelites, and others from the Levant. Unfortunately, there are no known documents because the Phoenicians typically wrote on papyrus, which rapidly degraded over time. However, historians can still piece together crucial elements of the legal system by examining clay tablets or references to the system in the documents of nearby civilizations. In general, the Phoenicians did not appear to differ much from other Levantine societies, preferring a biased and harsh legal system.

As with many other cultures that developed in the Levant, there was a somewhat codified system of laws and general practices that controlled behavior within the civilization. In general, the upper classes had the most rights in society, and laws were not always applied equally. People with money could typically escape punishment by paying fines instead of experiencing punishments, and it was not uncommon for a man to be able to deflect punishment to his wife, children, or slaves instead of on himself. For example, a man was able to send his family members and slaves to work in his stead if he had incurred a significant debt to another individual.

Laws were carried out by the state, and most legal matters were the responsibility of key administrators and rulers within the city-states. Being a lawyer did eventually become a profession but not at the outset. Instead, free men could represent themselves, while everyone else had to hope someone would plead their case for them. This made it difficult for women, underage youths, slaves, and indentured servants to receive justice.

Punishments tended to be severe, and they often focused on the concept of equal punishment for a crime. For example, if someone killed another's slave, their own slave would be executed. There were numerous major crimes that were illegal, including murder and theft. Rape tended to be a gray area. Men who raped were told to marry their victims and pay a sum of money to the father of the woman instead of facing any other punishment.

Prisons and jails did exist, but the Phoenicians used such institutions more as holding spaces before trials than as places for people to serve out sentences. It was much easier to impose a fine, punishment, or execution than it was to keep somebody alive for years. Unfortunately, out of the limited information modern audiences have on the Phoenicians, this is the majority of what is known about their legal system. It is clear that each city-state and colony would have its own bylaws, and there were also religious laws that needed to be fulfilled. All of this would affect the culture of Phoenician daily life in a variety of ways.

Chapter 4 – Daily Life

Although the courts were significant for merchants and the upper classes, they were not the only factors that determined the way of life for the majority. There were dozens of other social and cultural institutions responsible for controlling how the average individual was expected to conduct themselves and behave around others. The most significant, besides class, was gender. Men and women were assigned different roles that they were expected to adhere to at all times.

Gender Roles

As was typical among the cultures of the Levant, men were seen as the dominant gender and thus controlled law, politics, and the family. While upper-class men could be merchants, judges, senior officials, and participate in politics, the majority of the male population were poor farmers or occasionally craftsmen, laborers, carpenters, and other professions that required physical labor. Payment was often received as food, although money could change hands in the cities.

Only nobles were given full rights to participate in courts and assert their independence, but Phoenician men still had more rights than women. While they could not vote, they could legally own property, enter into contracts, and travel and trade on their own. They were responsible for the life and death of their wives and children, and they could even exert control over widowed mothers. There are some cases of Phoenician men selling their wives and children as labor to pay off debts, and men could have affairs without being punished unless they slept with another man's wife.

Women possessed few rights and were considered the property of their fathers and then their husbands. While many held jobs as laborers, weavers, and embroiderers, they were also expected to maintain households and bear and raise children. Contrary to popular belief, ancient Phoenician women, like many others in the Levant, engaged in backbreaking physical labor as farmers, construction workers, and miners, in addition to their domestic duties.

However, unlike men, they could never attain a position of power above a male counterpart. For example, a woman might be a laborer who helped build a house, but she could never be the foreman. Women also could not own property or enter into contracts, and they could not live by themselves even when widowed. They were expected to join the house of their nearest male relative, whether it be a son, brother, brother-in-law, or father. Upper-class women definitely had more rights than poor women but were still restricted and confined in their roles. Some learned to read and could exercise political influence, but they were still expected to be subservient to male relatives.

In Phoenician culture, there is an obvious Canaanite influence. Men were required to learn a trade between the ages of eleven and thirteen years old, while women remained at home and needed to care for their siblings and train under their mothers to become good wives and housekeepers. This meant understanding how to comb wool fibers and weave them into the fabric, sew, repair household items, cook, clean, bake, and also brew alcoholic beverages. Men, meanwhile, devoted their youth to becoming skilled in farming, shepherding, construction, or a similar profession that would support a family. Many learned additional skills like how to repair the tools of their trade, bartering in public markets, or basic accounting, like addition and subtraction.

Lower-class men and women would not have known how to read or write, and complex accounting was reserved for the nobility. Instead, most individuals would know basic mathematics, like simple addition. This did not mean the Phoenicians were dumb but rather that they lacked access to education. Upper-class men and women usually possessed some form of literacy, and complex counting and arithmetic were essential to learn for those who wanted to become a merchant and enter the great trading enterprises that characterized the economy. Unfortunately, most people would be simple laborers rather than wealthy participants in the industry.

As with most societies from the Levant, the Phoenicians also expected different sexual behaviors from the genders. Casual sex was frowned upon in Phoenician society, but men were still able to sleep with prostitutes, especially if the men were members of the upper classes. Women, on the other hand, needed to be virgins upon marriage and could only have sex with their husbands. While reproduction was the goal, some documents indicate that the Phoenicians also believed in sex for intimacy as a sign of a happy marriage. It is unclear whether the Phoenicians practiced polygamy like other Levantine civilizations.

Most marriages occurred when the man was around eighteen years old and the woman was closer to fifteen or sixteen. Although there were age gaps between couples and some women were married as young as twelve or thirteen, these were rare and were almost always noble marriages. In these cases, the wedding was arranged when the participants were children and would not be consummated until the bride and groom were closer to sixteen or seventeen years old. This was because the Phoenicians were aware that young women were unable to safely have children until they had grown older and developed wider hips.

Diet

The Phoenicians did not possess too much terrestrial territory but did acquire numerous foods from their trading partners in the Mediterranean Sea. The typical Phoenician diet thus tended to combine the natural foods of the Levant with some more unusual choices taken from around the sea. Some options included olives, wine, bread made from local grains, dried fish, garlic for flavor, lamb, goat, cheese, and even watermelon and grapes. Figs and dates were also local and could be used as a fresh treat to help even up the monotony of grains and assorted vegetables.

The Common Fig

The Phoenicians did not have enough land to cultivate large farms because of their coastal cities, so they tended to rely on traded goods as well as the seafood they could take from the Mediterranean. Their fresh-caught fish would have included tuna and mackerel, and there is some evidence to suggest the Phoenicians ate crustaceans and mussels as well. Spears and boats would have been ideal for fishing, and nets could be woven of rough fibers. Hunting did occur, and the Phoenicians ate local produce from cows, boars, and even horses. After all, they had little need of these land animals when almost all their trading was done by boat on the vast expanse of the Mediterranean.

While cities might have had professional bakers and brewers, a lot of resources were made at home by women. The baking of bread was a daily chore that took several hours of hard labor, during which women needed to grind up grains like rye into a powder before mixing them with yeast and water. Bread was typically made flat along the edges of large clay pots and eaten with a variety of locally grown and gathered herbs and vegetables. They usually couldn't cook huge batches of bread at once because of the lack of preservatives, meaning any extra would have moldered quickly.

Housing and Architecture

Phoenician architecture was reminiscent of that of their Canaanite ancestors. It was typified by large temples that possessed double-columned facades front and center. Visitors could ascend to the temples by climbing a short staircase and then entering enclosed sacred spaces. These spaces tended to be closed off to all but the most significant members of society, including the priests and royalty. Once inside, the spaces were characterized by cube-like shrines with open fronts. Besides the temples, it was common to encounter dams and artificial harbors, which were necessary to keep the seafaring civilization functioning properly.

Away from the harbors and temples, the settlements were surrounded by large fortification walls that were built high and thick. The most common materials used in the building of these walls were limestone pulled from quarries in the Levant and mudbrick made from nearby resources. Square towers and large gates dotted the surface, allowing individuals who brought goods and food from the countryside to enter and trade. Although the Phoenicians did possess quite a bit of agricultural land, the majority of the population lived in cities and were typically employed in businesses related to commerce.

Domestic buildings and housing tended to be quite modest, especially among the lower classes. Mudbrick was again the most common building material, especially since builders and families could make it on their own and then put it together. Most houses would be composed of a single story with one, two, or three rooms where the family and their livestock would live together. It was easier to create a roof out of rushes than any other material, although wealthier individuals could afford a timber model. The nobility had more choices and tended to live in two- or three-story homes. While merchants might have used a mudbrick or limestone model, most nobility and royals could have had an entirely stone home. Temples were additionally made of limestone and were frequently home to their priests and priestesses.

Beyond these basics, historians and archaeologists struggle to piece together greater trends about Phoenician architecture because much of the civilization's buildings were destroyed or sieged and taken by other empires. Much of the original designs, therefore, did not remain behind, leaving scholars to fill in the blanks and attempt to make statements about the overall character of the buildings. However, Phoenician architects seemed to prefer austerity, if clay tablets left by visiting Greek and Roman authors are any indication. Their buildings were plain compared to those of their neighbors but leaned toward having an opulent elegance that sparingly used decorative elements in favor of clean lines.

After doing some research on the local geography and the practicality of acquiring stone (it was not practical at all), archaeologists think that many buildings were constructed using wood from nearby abundant cedar forests, which would have supplied a durable material. The problem with this choice is that much of the material did not remain for posterity since wood degrades far faster than stone and cannot survive the vestiges of time. So, instead of having much knowledge about smaller, more common buildings, historians instead have a better understanding of what large public temples and gathering spaces would have looked like.

Urban housing, though, can be seen depicted in the paintings and murals of other societies like the ancient Greeks, who recorded most Phoenician homes as having two columns by the entryway and sometimes encompassing multiple floors. Domestic dwellings had ovens and basalt stones used by women to grind grain for beer and bread, and the corners were rounded for a more pleasing finish. Smaller buildings had grates that allowed access to public sewer systems to stop the flow of waste from making individuals sick. Mudbrick was used as the primary building material, although wealthier folk could afford stone and rare woods like olive, oak, and strawberry. There is almost no evidence of town planning in the overall design of cities because the Phoenicians were restrained by the confines of their territory, according to records.

One cannot discuss architecture without examining how a society cared for its dead. Phoenician tombs are remarkably intact and long-lasting, especially compared to housing and more temporary structures. The *tophet* played a central role in these tombs, as it was a sacrificial altar for animals—and potentially humans—where living beings would be killed and then burned to honor the gods and the deceased. The ashes were scraped from the flat surface of the *tophet* and placed in urns, which sometimes contained the ashes of people as well. These urns were sealed with stones and placed in the *tophet*, which could hold anywhere from five to twenty urns. These *tophets* were often built within shaft tombs, which were several meters deep and accessible through a vertical corridor. The majority of the population would be burned and placed in these shaft tombs, while richer families could afford personal tombs built into hillsides, which were accessible by stairs.

When it comes to shrines and temples, there appeared to be two styles. One was of a religious center placed in a natural clearing, typically near mountains, rivers, deep in the forests, or by stones that held significance to a particular deity. Such shrines might be decorated with boughs and flowers and had elements like the *tophet* but did not possess many permanent structures. Temples, on the other hand, were lavish and made from stone and sometimes marble. Columns were essential and featured styles borrowed from civilizations like the Assyrians, Egyptians, and Greeks.

Each temple had a sacred interior sanctum where only priests could go, as well as a storage area for religious relics. Libations could be made in the temple or by the entrance, and many featured thrones and symbolically carved wall reliefs for the deities they represented. The Phoenicians, unlike the Egyptians, Assyrians, and Greeks, seem to have prohibited the creation of large sculptural likenesses of their gods. Most gods and goddesses had individual temples rather than a single central location for worship, and all of the city-states had an accessible temple for the chief deity of that place.

Chapter 5 – Beauty and Apparel

Because the Phoenicians cultivated trade and social relationships, the merchants became perhaps the most influential portion of the population. Instead of forming companies like modern traders, these merchants tended to keep the business in the family and would form long-lasting partnerships with other families in desirable locations like Egypt. Men and women in this class were not required to participate in military service or dirty work like farming and thus cultivated a culture of beauty and style, commissioning the creation of elaborate tunics, necklaces, and hats. Other wealthy nobles adopted this style, and clothing and accessories became the best way to tell just how important and influential people were.

Male Clothing

Social class determined the style of male Phoenician clothing, although there were general overarching trends. For common individuals, men could be expected to wear a close-fitting tunic that stretched from the waist to just above the knee. Linen or cotton was the preferred material because it was light and helped working men withstand the heat along the Mediterranean Sea. Ornamentation or embroidery was lacking because of the cost of the thread, and jewelry was not common. Most men would wear a round or conical headdress with a topknot that gave the top a spherical appearance. All individuals wore sandals.

Upper-class men wore similar clothing but with more finery and detail. Their tunic, called a *shenti*, often featured sewn patterns and embroidery to denote a man's rank. The front parted to reveal an underlying piece of fabric to give more detail to the waist. Adorned lappets also decorated the front, and girdles were popular. Over the underlying *shenti* could be worn another close-fitting tunic that clung to the shoulders and upper arms. While some archaeologists in the past have described it as being similar to a modern jersey, it looks closer to a woman's bolero jacket that ends underneath the bust line.

When not following the style of a *shenti* and shoulder jacket, a wealthy or important man could wear an interior robe that reached the feet. Over it would be an outer blouse or shirt that descended to just above the knees. If they didn't wear this blouse, they could instead have a mantle thrown over their left shoulder, which would follow the man like a cape as he moved. Most men would, once again, have a conical hat with a topknot, although these headdresses were far more elaborate than those of lower-class men.

Priests were a separate class but still shared many similar elements to their secular peers. Their headdresses, for example, had topknots but also narrow crowns covered in the representations of bull heads. Their main tunic was a long robe that stretched from the base of the neck to the feet. Over the robe was a mantle that covered the right arm and shoulder and went down to the right knee. Detailed ornamentation decorated each piece of clothing, and embroidery was common around the collar and hem of the robe.

Hair, especially facial hair, was of the utmost importance to a Phoenician man because it denoted cleanliness and their position in society. Most men kept their hair underneath a cap and did not brush it often. When the cap was taken off, the hair tended to be a curly mess, although men liked to style it so that one or two rows of curls dangled from underneath the rim of the headdress. Many historians compare Phoenician beards to those of the Assyrians because men of both cultures tended to style it either as three to five rows of tight curls or as one long curly mass. Mustaches were not common and appeared to be shaved off in favor of long beards.

Ornaments for Men

The most common male accessory was the collar, which was worn around the neck and tended to be made of three rows of precious metals. These resembled Egyptian collars and were worn primarily by elites who could afford hammered gold. The collar extended from the throat down to the breast and was frequently complemented with armlets, bracelets, and rings for the fingers. Armlets tended to be the plainest of ornamentation, often being a piece of twisted metal that looped once or twice around the upper arm. Bracelets were similar but could occasionally include precious stones and agates. Rings were popular among all classes, but the best were made of silver or gold, had an inset stone, and often were used as seals for closing documents.

One well-known example of male jewelry comes from the rule of Etyander, a king of Paphos. Archaeologists discovered his armlets, which were made of small, single twists of gold that barely touched at the ends. They were bare except for a single inscription: "Eteadoro to Papo basileos," which in English means, "The property of Etyander, King of Paphos." While plain, everyone still knew that the jewelry conveyed power and respect.

Scholars do not know whether men often wore necklaces. Most artwork depicts women wearing the traditional three or four strands, but men are less frequently seen with such jewelry. Many educated historians believe men did wear necklaces based on the data currently possessed about European, Asian, and African fashions of the time. Jewelry was often used culturally to depict social status, with the wealthiest individuals often draping themselves in fine pieces made of gold and jewels. So, while there is little evidence about men possessing necklaces, it is very likely that they did.

Female Clothing

Although female goddesses were often depicted nude, Phoenician women were carefully garbed head to foot for modesty. While men had tight tunics, female robes were meant to be loose and worn in deliberately placed folds. The only points of interest were typically around the bust and waist, where it was acceptable to have some shape before the fabric became billowy and created heavy folds of drapery. Girdles were used to give the material definition and were tied in the front. Petticoats were common and typically went underneath the robes. Women wore leather sandals to protect their feet from sand, rocks, and other hazards.

Hair was an unusual case for women. Although women from some regions wore caps to hide their locks for modesty, others wore theirs loose in waves that parted at the center of the head. Hair tended to be shoulder length and could be kept in check with a single woven or leather band. Others used loose hoods, which also protected one's face from the sun. Typically, wealthier women were more likely to have styled hair with bands, while lower-class individuals covered their heads to help prevent sunburns. Because of the natural heat in the city-states, Phoenician women avoided growing their hair longer than their shoulders.

Ornaments for Women

Phoenician women wore many more ornaments and accessories than their male counterparts. Jewelry and ornamentation demonstrated familial wealth and social status, and thus, merchants, royals, and the daughters and wives of noble families were the most decorated. Excavations made in Phoenician territories reveal hundreds of rings, necklaces, bracelets, armlets, earrings, regular finger rings, brooches, lockets, buckles, and even buttons made of precious materials and jewels. Even some toiletries were made of these components, especially mirrors.

Necklaces

Necklaces are an interesting ornament among the Phoenicians and were considered a necessary part of their attire. However, archaeologists believe many of the artifacts uncovered belonged to the nobility because of their presence in tombs and royal graves, so it is unlikely the average Phoenician wore opulent strands. Instead, a commoner most likely possessed necklaces with colored clay beads that had multiple strands layered to beautiful effect.

Women are believed to have worn three to four layers of necklaces at once layered over each other. The first layer wrapped around the neck, similar to a choker, and rested right below the chin. The second necklace would be slightly more ornate and ended where the chest began, usually right around the collarbone. The third and fourth strands were much longer and tended to feature ornate ornaments made of glass, gold, crystal, and other precious stones. Many pendants were shaped after natural elements like pomegranates, acorns, and lotus flowers. Geometric shapes were also possible, especially cones and vases.

Beads adorned all of these layers. These beads could be made of clay for the lower classes, while upper-class individuals typically had large beads made of gold or glass. Precious stones were occasionally used to make beads, but these were rare. A short necklace might have between fifty to sixty beads, while a long strand could have over one hundred. Beads were often interspersed with bugles made of carnelian or onyx, and jewelry that came from Egypt often had oval beads made of blue or bluish-green glass. These beads typify a material called "Egyptian blue," which was made using a specific chemical process during firing and became a staple of trade between the Egyptians and Phoenicians.

Gold Necklace with Pendants, c. 900 BCE

Several necklaces that survived the decay of time come from the ladies of Cyprus. The first has a row of 103 gold beads in a pattern of alternating spheres and ovals. The oval beads are connected to gold pendants made to look like lotus blossoms, while the central pendant is a woman's head and bust in the Egyptian style. The attention to detail is clear in the workmanship, and the necklace itself is heavy. Another Cyprus piece has 64 beads. Twenty-two of the beads are larger than the rest and are affixed to eighteen pendants with delicate gold flowers.

Although tastes vary, an elegant example of Phoenician craftsmanship is a necklace made with a woven solid gold cord that was hammered and shaped to be soft and elastic. At either end of the necklace are caps to protect the cord. One side features a wrought lion's head with a ring in its mouth, while the other end has a hook to form a complete clasp. Archaeologists have been fascinated by this piece for years due to its quality, with one writing, "In this arrangement, in the curves of the thin wire, which folds back upon itself again and again, there is an air of ease, an apparent negligence, which is the very perfection of technical skill."

Other Jewelry

Women cultivated a fashion focused on opulent designs and extra ornamentation that depicted one's social class and frivolous wealth, and bracelets were a popular choice because of their visibility. Phoenician upper-class women often wore many varieties, with gold being the most common. Some bracelets were bands of solid gold without ornamentation. These could weigh anywhere between 200 and 300 grams (between a little over 7 and 10.5 ounces), which made then ornate and heavy around the wrist. Others were open designs meant to be worn around the upper arm. These did not meet at the ends but did often have designs along the ends like the heads of lions or bulls. If there were decorations, they tended to be elaborate carvings and decorations in floral patterns or depictions of the Phoenician alphabet.

Earrings were donned by men and women alike and could be as some of the most creative pieces, ranging from simple and sterile to curious and downright fanciful. Some were connected with chains to make elegant suspended patterns, others featured large medallions, and still others were shaped to resemble human heads. In general, the Phoenicians favored earrings that had a ring inserted in the ear, followed by long central chains that connected to one another and suspended long amulets or decorations representative of something significant. These were frequently the symbols of deities, small vases, or animals.

One visitor to the Museum of New York took the time to view a collection brought from Cyprus and described in lush detail the lavish nature of Phoenician earrings:

> An entirely different type is that furnished by an ear-ring in the Museum of New York brought from Cyprus, where the loop of the ornament rises from a sort of horse-shoe, patterned with bosses and spirals, and surrounded by a rough edging of knobs, standing at a little distance one from

another. Other forms found also in Cyprus are the ear-ring with the long pendant, which has been called "an elongated pear," ornamented towards the lower end with small blossoms of flowers, and terminating in a minute ball, which recalls the "drops" that are still used by the jewellers of our day; the loop which supports a *crux ansata*; that which has attached to it a small square box, or measure containing a heap of grain, thought to represent wheat; and those which support fruit of various kinds. An ear-ring of much delicacy consists of a twisted ring, curved into a hook at one extremity, and at the other ending in the head of a goat, with a ring attached to it, through which the hook passes. Another, rather curious than elegant, consists of a double twist, ornamented with lozenges, and terminating in triangular points finely granulated.[9]

Earrings were thus one of the most complicated yet desired accessories by far, although women also took great care when it came to their toiletries, buckles, and brooches. Phoenician ladies needed to fasten their dresses with buckles, but they favored simple metals over decoration for the sake of convenience. Wealthy women instead spent their fortunes on circular mirrors with metal backs, crystal vases, gold funnels, and even gold perfume bottles. Although these were not seen by the public, they were items that signified wealth and power that were enjoyed in the privacy of homes.

[9] George Rawlinson, *The Great Empires of the Ancient East: Egypt, Phoenicia, Parthia, Chaldea, Assyria, Media, Babylon, Persia, Sasanian Empire, Israel, and Judah*. Oxfordshire, 1906.

Chapter 6 – An Unwritten Early History

The Phoenicians left little behind, but they did leave clues in the earth for modern archaeologists and scholars to discover. For much of the 18th and 19th centuries, people relied on religious texts and historical documents from the Greeks, Romans, Egyptians, and Assyrians to catch a glimpse of this massive seafaring civilization. This poses several major problems. First, they are all inherently biased as they were developed by rival civilizations who benefited from making the Phoenicians look good or bad depending on their current trade agreements. Second, contemporary historians cannot use religious texts as factual sources, especially since they have been translated and rewritten numerous times over the last 2,000 years.

This trend of using such unreliable sources has changed in recent decades as ongoing archaeological excavations in Lebanon, Tunisia, the Iberian Peninsula, and the rest of the Mediterranean have resulted in significant material evidence to explain various elements of the Phoenician civilization. Artifacts are considered material culture, and with material culture, scholars can study a time period, civilization, or society by looking at the kinds of goods they manufactured and used in their regular lives.

A major downfall of this approach is that the most common items a civilization uses frequently disintegrate and are lost to time because they were made from cheap materials or due to the fact that nobody saved them because of their plainness. However, one benefit of studying ancient civilizations through material culture is how groups like the Phoenicians buried items with their dead. These grave goods could be jewelry and symbols of wealth, but they were more often things used by people, like combs, mirrors, dishes, and similar objects.

Through archaeological expeditions conducted under the auspices of institutions like the National Museum of Beirut, the American University of Beirut, and the British Museum, modern scholars now have access to this material culture and have started to construct a history of the Phoenicians, albeit one that is rough and lacks details about certain city-states or elements of daily life. For context, the world knows more about World War II, which lasted for seven years, than it does about the Phoenicians, who were around for over one thousand years.

Early history is the most difficult to piece together for a plethora of reasons. First and foremost is the development of technology. Older civilizations wrote on clay or mud tablets that could be erased and rewritten upon. If someone wanted to preserve a tablet, they could harden it over a fire. These tablets did not decay from exposure to the sun or air, and thus, they could survive. As a fun fact, one massive library of clay tablets, which was burned in order to destroy it, actually survived the blaze with hundreds of tablets intact that modern audiences can still view.

Unfortunately, the Phoenicians did not use clay tablets. By the time they arrived on the scene, society had already developed papyrus. Wanting to keep an edge on their competitors, enjoying access to the raw materials needed to make it, and liking the lightness of the paper, the Phoenicians thus turned to papyrus to keep records. The major problem with this is that papyrus degrades rapidly, especially when exposed to air, water, and the sun. So, there are few written records left by the Phoenicians.

Another issue in trying to put together an early history is that the Phoenicians emerged toward the end of the Bronze Age, around a time known as the Bronze Age Collapse. They had barely distinguished themselves from their ancestors, the Canaanites, when the Near Eastern society suddenly collapsed. The Bronze Age Collapse could have been triggered by a variety of phenomena—scholars still debate to this day on how it actually occurred—including environmental issues like droughts, famine, overextended resource usage, and the arrival of a mysterious force called the Sea Peoples. These Sea Peoples are referenced in documents across several situations and appear to have been a seafaring people that arrived on the eastern coast of the Mediterranean and went to work butchering and slaughtering other peoples.

An Egyptian Image Representing the Sea Peoples

As one can imagine, this unrest led to the loss of many records. Civilizations were derailed, and societies were forced to regroup and reform. The Phoenicians moved to a region of the Levant that was relatively untouched and continued to build their own society, taking advantage of the chaos to claim some viable land and an advantageous spot on the sea. Without so much unrest, would it have been possible for the Phoenicians to get an edge over nearby powers like the Canaanites, Hittites, and Egyptians? Probably not.

Phoenician history can be divided into several different periods that explain what the overall theme or trend was in their civilization. These include:

- The Late Bronze Age (1550 to 1200 BCE)
- Iron Age I (1200 to 900 BCE)
- Iron Age II (900 to 586 BCE)
- Babylonian Period (586 to 539 BCE)
- Persian Period (539 to 332 BCE)
- Hellenistic Period (332 to 63 BCE)
- Roman Period (63 BCE to 324 CE)

These periods demonstrate when the Phoenicians first emerged as a distinct culture, when they started to become an independent power, their golden age, their subjugation under the Assyrians, becoming vassals of the Babylonians, then serving the Persians, the conquest of Alexander the Great, and their eventual fall to Greek and Roman influence and power. Throughout this time, the society and culture of the Phoenicians underwent numerous changes, especially in terms of technology, trading power, artistry, and political structure. However, only a few of these developments are left for posterity.

The Late Bronze Age

The Phoenician story begins when they were just starting to distinguish themselves from their predecessors and cousins, the Canaanites. Around this time, the native peoples of the Levant started to gravitate toward large coastal cities that offered opportunities for wealth, security, regular work, and culture. Some of the largest were Byblos and Tyre, which would go on to become two of the most successful Phoenician city-states. Individuals in these urban centers carved a niche for themselves by becoming intermediaries in the trade between Egypt and the nearby Syrian states, helping to form the tradition of the Phoenicians as traders.

However, it can be difficult to distinguish when Canaanites started to become Phoenicians. Could someone be a Canaanite and a Phoenician? Could someone be a Phoenician yet still be a Canaanite? The definite answer is sort of. Being Phoenician required having Canaanite heritage, living in the Near Eastern region, and participating in a new twist on religion and language. Someone could be a Canaanite and a Phoenician, but it would be difficult for a Phoenician to not be a Canaanite.

Before c. 1230 BCE, the Canaanites were in their own golden age, which is a term that refers to when culture, trade, and society flourish. This came to a grinding halt during the Bronze Age Collapse when a mysterious force decimated the city of Ugarit, leaving the region abandoned. At the same time, the nearby Israelites invaded and attempted to take arable farmland, while the mysterious Sea Peoples from the west arrived and started laying waste to anyone who stood in the way of total conquest. The Philistines moved in, claiming southern Canaanite cities as their territory.

To add fuel to the fire, the Near East experienced a surge of unfavorable environmental factors, including a prolonged drought. The ensuing famine led many to abandon cities in search of natural resources like wild vegetation and fresh water. The political structure of the central city died out, leaving the Canaanites to become more nomadic. The ensuing chaos called for a complete reordering of society, and when the dust fell, a new power known as Phoenicia emerged from the Canaanite survivors, becoming an independent region on the coast.

Iron Age I

Unfortunately, few sources remain to inform modern scholars about life in Phoenicia during the 12th century BCE, although some evidence indicates the cities of Byblos and Sidon were able to rapidly recover from the economic devastation of the Bronze Age Collapse. These cities would become central to the power of the Phoenician civilization since they were economic juggernauts and had access to desirable land and water trade routes. At the same time, Sidon started to distinguish itself as a military powerhouse, and Arwad arrived on the scene as well, sporting an impressive number of chariots.

The first textual source to discuss the Iron Age Phoenicians is an account of Assyrian King Tiglath-Pileser I's campaign against the Phoenicians sometime between 1114 and 1076 BCE. Tiglath-Pileser I desired the abundant cedar forests controlled by the Phoenicians and launched ground-based military sieges against Byblos and Sidon. The king records how he managed to exact tribute from the leaders of these cities. Tyre was around at this point, but it was deemed too insignificant to add to the record.

The next main source about the Phoenicians was created by Wen-Amon, a senior Egyptian official from Thebes who worked at the temple of Amon-Ra. He traveled along the coast to procure cedar wood for the construction of a new holy barge, and he mentions that Byblos and Sidon were considered some of the most impressive coastal cities and powers of the time. Tyre is mentioned but was again thought of as insignificant in the power structure of the Mediterranean world. Wen-Amon's account hails from 1075 to 1060 BCE, indicating the sieges of Tiglath-Pileser I might not have been as effective as he had claimed.

Of particular importance was that Byblos and Sidon were in such an advantageous position that when Wen-Amon arrived and demanded cedar wood, the Phoenicians were able to negotiate instead of handing over tribute. The prince of Byblos, Zakar-Baal, told the official that Egypt needed to pay first before they would receive the wood. Because Byblos had previously been subservient to the Egyptian empire, the ability to request money before goods were given was impressive. This demonstrates how Egyptian power was in decline while the Phoenicians were on the rise.

Piecing together the exact history of the ensuing 11th century BCE is difficult, as there are fewer personal accounts and inscriptions and more vague references in the broad histories of civilizations like Egypt. Religious texts, like the biblical books of Joshua, Judges, and Samuel, start to use the term "Sidonian" at this point in time to indicate someone who could be Phoenician. There are a few reasons why this could have been, but the fact that Sidon was built near arable agricultural land did give the urban center an advantage. Tyre, after all, was trapped on an island.

Sidon's rise to power proved to change the overall Phoenician political structure. While the Phoenicians originally sided with Egypt as their default trading partner, Sidon had no interest in doing so. Instead, Sidon directed its attention to the nearby Syrian power, which was growing and proved to be a closer and more reliable trading partner. This was bad news for Tyre, who relied on Egyptian purchases of goods like cedar wood to afford to keep the people of the island city fed and commercially successful.

Iron Age II

Unfortunately for Sidon, its power did not last into the 10th century BCE. Tyre's golden age began when Hiram I (c. 969 to 936 BCE) ascended the throne. He shifted the balance of power toward Tyre by systematically exploiting nearby pan-Mediterranean trade routes. Hiram I worked to achieve a maritime monopoly and succeeded by employing a fleet capable of traveling up and down the Levantine coast to transport imports and exports and also beat off rivals through naval power.

Toward the end of the 12th century BCE, a new city-state emerged as the most powerful: Tyre. Although previously ignored because it struggled to chisel its way into commerce, something changed that allowed Tyre to subsume the position of Byblos and Sidon. Tyre became urbanized and followed the new developments in the making of pottery, which necessitated craftsmen and women to settle down and work in the cities to produce this profitable item.

Tyre also adopted new commercial partners, deciding to make deals with nearby Israel. These two states underwent joint trading ventures to acquire gold and fed off of one another's strengths. In particular, Tyre gave Israel more access to the coast, while Israel allowed Tyre to have some control over overland trade routes that went deeper into Asia. Tyre could now manage the flow of goods from Syria down to Egypt, enacting taxes and only allowing traders on their own terms. It also gave the city-state access to spices and precious metals like silver and gold, which arrived from Arabia.

Hiram I's alliances could not last for long, though. King Solomon's Kingdom of Israel divided into Judah and Israel because of rival political claimants, and the Phoenician king needed to find a more stable and reliable trading partner rather than trying to get the two Israelite states to work together. Tyre thus had to reevaluate its political decisions and started to ease away from Israel and Judah, choosing to cooperate with nearby Phoenician city-states and turning south to North Africa.

Tyre underwent a brief lull in its success but managed to enter a second golden age through the coronation of Ithobaal I (ruled 887 to 856 BCE). Ithobaal's interests lay with territorial conquest. In over a decade, he managed to acquire and control so much territory that he declared himself the "King of the Sidonians," a title that would be adopted by his successors in Tyre for centuries to come. The title also appeared in the Greek Homeric poems and in the religious books of the Old Testament.

Ithobaal I combined Tyre with the territory of nearby Sidon, creating the first hints of a single Phoenician state. He labeled Tyre as the capital and went on to establish perhaps the first Phoenician colonies: Auza in Libya and Botrys, north of Byblos. These colonies were designed to add additional precious natural resources to the Tyrian commercial networks, including copper and other metals. Ithobaal would go on to create a colony on Cyprus as well.

However, Tyre's success once again came under fire, this time by the Assyrians. The Assyrian Empire was a nearby Asian juggernaut. The Phoenicians long existed on the fringes of this civilization, avoiding the numerous Assyrian military excursions by paying tribute. In fact, Tyre often took advantage of Assyrian conquests by claiming territory that was disrupted by warfare and chaos. Tyre's success changed, however, when the Assyrians crowned Shalmaneser III (ruled 859 to 824 BCE) as king.

Chapter 7 – Vassal to the Empires

While it is simple to divide the early years of the Phoenicians by technological age, the latter years are best understood by figuring out which great empire the city-states had become subservient to. Although the Phoenicians were an economic powerhouse, they exerted little military might. Clustered on the coast and with a small natural population, the city-states were repeatedly forced to submit to the much larger and more powerful empires that swept across the Levant and that boasted massive tracts of land in Asia, Africa, and Europe. The first of these empires was the Assyrians.

Vassalage to the Assyrian Empire

King Shalmaneser III rose to power in 858 BCE and ascended to the throne with plans of conquest. As soon as he gathered his military forces, he began an aggressive campaign throughout northern Syria and southern Anatolia. One of his primary targets were the Phoenician city-states along the coast of the Mediterranean Sea, which he subjugated over a period of three years. The Phoenicians were now forced to pay an inordinate amount of tribute to the

Assyrians in payments that consisted of money and physical goods and resources.

At this point in time, the Phoenicians could be considered vassals of the more powerful Assyrian Empire. In political terms, a vassal is a country that is subordinate to another and engages in a relationship wherein one pays tribute to another to avoid being invaded or attacked. However, being a vassal of the Assyrians was not an unpleasant situation for the Phoenicians, who managed to garner a favorable position among the numerous vassals in the Middle East.

Unlike some of the other states in the region, the Phoenicians were treated well by Shalmaneser III, who remembered that city-states like Tyre cooperated with his father and did not plot to rebel. The geopolitical importance of the Phoenicians was further beneficial for Assyria, who needed the city-states to conduct diplomacy around the Mediterranean and continue to serve as a source of income for the ever-expanding empire. In this way, Phoenicia was able to bargain for its city-states' sanctity with its economic resources and trading authority. The Assyrians also feared the Phoenicians might fall into the hands of their rivals, the Egyptians.

Even after Shalmaneser III died in 824, the Phoenician city-states were still able to maintain a state of semi-independence. Shalmaneser III's successors did not want to interfere in the internal affairs of Phoenicia, which allowed the city-states to maintain a limited level of independence.

Unfortunately, this luck would run out around 744 BCE. At this point, Tiglath-Pileser III rose to the Assyrian throne and immediately began numerous far-reaching campaigns into the Levant. As part of the campaigns, the recently crowned ruler sought to put an end to the various independent states in the region and make their territory part of the expanding Assyrian Empire. This meant that the Phoenician city-states, particularly Tyre, became targets.

After several years of battles, the entirety of the Levant submitted to Assyrian authority in 738 BCE. The cities on the northern

Phoenician coast were annexed into the empire, while southern city-states like Tyre and Byblos managed to remain as tributaries. However, they were no longer allowed to operate under a system of relative political and economic independence and had to run their decisions by Tiglath-Pileser and his administrators.

However, Tyre was not pleased with the situation. Just a year after the annexation, the king of Tyre chose to ally himself with an anti-Assyrian coalition in the Levant. Tiglath-Pileser responded by mustering his forces and sweeping down the Phoenician coast, crushing the opposition. Seeing the way the wind was blowing, Tyre immediately surrendered and offered tribute. Tiglath-Pileser accepted and left, demonstrating that the continued economic success of the Phoenician city was more important to him than crushing the city for its insolence.

Although not destroyed, Tyre still suffered. Assyria installed inspectors and market officials in the harbors of Tyre, eliminating economic and political independence. The subsequent kings were also required to pay 150 talents of gold a year to Assyria, a sum the equivalent of $150,000,000—if not more. Tyre paid the tribute for several years and then rebelled again, this time allying with nearby Sidon. The war lasted for two to three years, at which point the Phoenician city-states were captured and subjugated yet again.

The Assyrian monarch Sennacherib invaded the outlying territories of Tyre in 701 BCE, forcing the king to flee to Cyprus. The alliance between Tyre and Sidon was crushed, and Tyre lost control of nearby Sidon, as well as the majority of its population to Assyria. Thousands of residents were deported to the capital of Nineveh, and the coastal harbors were blockaded. Future blockades were established by generations of following Assyrian kings like Esarhaddon (681-669 BCE) and Ashurbanipal (669-631 BCE). By 640 BCE, all of mainland Tyre became an Assyrian province.

However, Assyrian dominance in the Levant would not last. On the rise was a new threat: the Babylonians. The Assyrian Empire became the victim of the Babylonian expansionist policy, and the Assyrians blindly allied themselves with their old enemy, the Egyptians, to try to retain control of the Levant and all of the Phoenician city-states. Unfortunately, the combined forces of Assyria and Egypt were not enough to stave off the Babylonians, who defeated both empires at Carchemish in 605 BCE.

Dominance by the Babylonians

The Babylonians were one of the most ancient peoples in known history, having developed around the city of Babylon in the 19th century BCE. The state of Babylon underwent numerous changes and waves of power throughout its lifetime, at one point being a great empire before being reduced to a small state controlled by the Assyrians. Although the Babylonians were subjugated by and paid tribute to the Assyrians from 911 to circa 612 BCE, their moment would come again. When the famous Assyrian ruler Ashurbanipal died and left a power vacuum, the Babylonians saw their chance and freed themselves from the shackles of vassalage, rebelling and forming the Neo-Babylonian Empire.

It was the Neo-Babylonian Empire that laid claim to Phoenician territory next. In the very first year of his long reign, Neo-Babylonian King Nebuchadnezzar II (605-562 BCE) began military campaigns throughout Syria with the intention of capturing and subjugating influential Assyrian territories. When he arrived on the Phoenician coast, the majority of the city-states understood which way the wind was blowing. Most immediately renounced their allegiance to the Assyrians and instead sent tribute to the Babylonians.

An Onyx Etching of Nebuchadnezzar II, c. 580 BCE

Tyre, however, once again rebelled. The city-state's fierce resistance resulted in a thirteen-year siege from 586 BCE until 573 BCE when the city council was forced to acknowledge defeat and surrender. The actions of the leaders had disastrous results for the citizens of Tyre. Tyre was reduced in power, and the king at the time, Ithobaal III, was sent to Babylon in captivity. A puppet ruler was installed before being replaced by a government full of Babylonian judges who ruled using their own justice system.

The once-powerful Tyre was now reduced in status among the Phoenician city-states and no longer boasted a strong military, navy, or economic success. Sidon immediately stepped into Tyre's place, essentially usurping the city's commercial contacts and natural resources. Sidon became the most prosperous Phoenician city and held this position for many years until Alexander the Great arrived and kicked it down.

Under Babylonian rule, life in Phoenicia was difficult. Commercial ventures diminished greatly, and much of the wealth of the cities instead went to line the coffers of the Neo-Babylonian monarchy. The Babylonian annexation of strategic regions, like southern Palestine, cut the Phoenicians off from their strategic trade routes, and Nebuchadnezzar II stole the cedar trade. Phoenicians were considered second-class citizens and were often subjected to Babylonian law and "encouraged" to follow Babylonian religious practices.

Things would not improve for the Phoenicians until after Nebuchadnezzar II's death. The new monarchs were not as effective as their predecessor and became distracted by the rise of yet another empire on the horizon: the Persians. King Nabonidus reinstated all of the original Phoenician royal lines in an attempt to garner the loyalty of the city-states, but it was not enough. Cyrus the Great was coming, and he would not be stopped.

The Achaemenid Empire

An Etching of Cyrus the Great

The above image of Cyrus the Great was created by copying a stone statue of the famous Persian leader from one of his numerous building projects. Cyrus ruled from 559 BCE until 530 BCE and managed to conquer Sippar and the city of Babylon later in his military conquests. This disrupted Babylonian power in the Levant, allowing the Phoenicians to exert some more influence at home. Cyrus actually treated the Phoenicians quite favorably, seemingly recognizing that their naval power and commercial contacts could be beneficial to his envisioned empire.

Under the Persians, the Phoenicians found a new purpose. They became the naval backbone of Cyrus the Great on the Mediterranean Sea and entered a prosperous period that lasted throughout the majority of the Achaemenid period. All four of the major Phoenician city-states (Tyre, Sidon, Byblos, and Arwad) were able to reinstate their monarchies and dynastic rule. They expanded physically and economically, claiming territory in the Levant as it came under the control of the Achaemenid Persians.

Initially, the Phoenician city-states were clustered into a single satrapy, or administrative district, which was under Persian control. The satrapy was called Athura, or Assyria. When Darius I took control from 522 BCE to 486 BCE, he subdivided the district into separate provinces to better control the flow of wealth and politics.

Control under the Persians could be considered perhaps one of the last golden ages for the Phoenician city-states. They found a tremendous niche serving as commercial backers and rulers of a massive portion of the Persian navy. Some Greek accounts even attest that the Phoenicians were the formidable navy commanders of Xerxes, who would traverse the Mediterranean and wage war with the ancient Greek city-states.

Unfortunately, prosperity never lasts in history. The final years of the 5th century BCE brought growing unrest for the Persians, who did not have strong rulers or an efficient administration. The territory began to fragment, and rebellions sprang up. Mainland Greece, Egypt, and western Asia Minor were some of the first locations to shirk Persian rule, and the Phoenicians grew antsy watching their influential trading partners leave. Sensing the growing weakness of the Persian state, the Phoenicians decided to leave.

At this point, people can probably guess which city-state rebelled first. The monarchs of Tyre saw an opportunity to leave and joined an anti-Persian alliance that included Egypt, Cyprus, and Athens. The alliance attacked Persia with all of its might but was decisively defeated in a naval battle in 381 BCE. In time, other city-states also rebelled against the Persians, including the powerful Sidon. Unfortunately for Sidon, the new Persian ruler, Artaxerxes III, was much more formidable than his predecessors. He led a massive army to quell the revolt in Sidon. By 344 BCE, all of the Phoenician city-states were back in Persian hands.

However, there was yet another conqueror on the horizon.

The Arrival of the Macedonians

While still under the control of the Persians, Phoenicia would be faced by another conqueror interested in the acquisition of their territories and the luxury goods they controlled. This would be the Macedonian Greeks, who were led by the famous Alexander the Great, a king who was no older than his early twenties by the time he marched upon Tyre in 332 BCE. Due to its position, Alexander was unable to attack the city directly from the sea, and it was too heavily walled along the land to be captured quickly. Instead, Alexander started a siege and ordered his men and captured slaves to build a causeway that was one kilometer long (a little over half a mile) to the island where Tyre was situated.

Alexander the Great

This causeway was built on a small natural land bridge that was less than two meters deep (a little over six and a half feet), making it the only realistic opportunity the Macedonians possessed to attack the city.[10] There was little the Phoenicians could do to delay destruction besides trying to stone or shoot the construction workers as they neared Tyre's walls. Eventually, it was completed, and the Macedonian artillery closed in upon the city. Some of the remains still exist in the region since the entire walkway was built of stone.

Because the water near the city was deeper than the rest, Alexander the Great could not bring his causeway straight to the walls. Instead, Alexander was forced to build two towers nearby that measured around 50 meters (160 feet) tall. The construction of the towers was delayed repeatedly by attacks from Tyre as well as the Tyrian navy, but the moving artillery platforms were soon completed. Catapults were built on top to attack the Tyrian wall defenders, while ballistas were added below to hurl rocks at the navy's ships and the lower portions of the walls. These towers and platforms were made of wood, which was easier to carry than stone, and they were covered

[10] Stephen English, *The Sieges of Alexander the Great* (Wiltshire: Pen & Sword Books Ltd., 2010).

with treated rawhide so the Phoenicians could not destroy them with flaming arrows.

The Tyrians were determined not to be beaten by the towers. Although the Macedonian platforms were the largest of their kind by that point in history, the Phoenicians used an old ship for transporting horses and devised a plan. They filled it with a variety of combustible substances, including sulfur, pitch, and dried branches. They then attached hanging cauldrons full of oil along the masts so they would fall when the masts burned down. They weighed down the back of the ship so the front tipped upward and then sent it directly at the towers before lighting it on fire.

The boat crashed into the towers, and the flames spread fast, burning up along the massive platforms. The cauldrons of oil fell with spectacular splashes, sending fire in every direction. The Macedonians were disoriented, and the siege equipment rapidly burned down. Afterward, members of the Tyrian navy swarmed the manmade pier and destroyed everything that came within their grasp, including the remaining equipment and the Macedonian soldiers and slaves who tried to douse the fires.

Alexander was daunted and delayed, but he was not finished. He desired Tyre. After careful consideration, he became convinced that the only way to capture the Phoenician city was through the use of an accomplished navy. Unfortunately for the Phoenicians, he had one because of his previous conquests of other Phoenician city-states that had been controlled by the Persians, including Arwad, Byblos, and Sidon. Through the acquisition of Persian vessels, Alexander had a fleet of eighty strong ships. These were then joined by 120 war galleys sent by Cyprus, whose king wished to join Alexander, potentially as a way to avoid being dominated himself. Ionia in Greece sent another 23, leaving Alexander with an impressive fleet of 223 ships ready for combat. The Tyrian navy possessed no hope of victory.

Alexander sailed upon Tyre and blockaded the ports through which supplies reached the city. Slower vessels were refitted with battering rams, but they had to be removed because Tyre had placed massive underwater blocks of stone to block rams many years before. The rams were anchored near the walls instead, but the Tyrians sent out divers to cut them off. Alexander then replaced the ropes with chains. The Tyrians tried to launch another counterattack, but they were unsuccessful. The Macedonian rams broke through the walls while its navy decimated the Phoenician ships, ending the siege in an absolute bloodbath and massacre.

Once Alexander captured Tyre, he was draconian. He killed 6,000 fighting men and crucified 2,000 of its leading citizens on the beach. He then allowed the king to remain in power, but he murdered much of the royal family and anyone who opposed the Macedonians. The city was sacked, the citizens were beaten in the streets, and women were captured and raped by the soldiers. Over 30,000 Tyrians were taken as slaves for the Macedonian army. After such a brutal display of power, many of the other Phoenician city-states acquiesced to Macedonian rule without a fight, fearful of what might happen if they resisted.

When Alexander the Great perished in 323 BCE, Phoenicia became divided between several of the following empires created by Alexander's successors, although the majority was controlled by the Ptolemaic dynasty of Egypt. Between 286 and 197 BCE, the Ptolemies reduced the influence of Phoenicia over the trading routes of the Eastern Mediterranean and installed high priests of Astarte as vassal rulers throughout the region. This caused tremendous cultural backlash and a significant economic downturn in Phoenicia, which struggled to thrive and continue its culture with the influence of Persia, Greece, and Egypt.

Chapter 8 – Trade and the Economy

The Phoenicians were among the greatest traders of the ancient world, capable of controlling massive networks of goods across the Mediterranean Sea, east into Asia, and down into Africa. Most of their prosperity could be attributed to the skills of their merchants, who ruled over the seas with an iron fist and superior technology. They established numerous commercial outposts designed to be reachable by ships that needed to dock between journeys to replenish their supplies and sell goods to a variety of civilizations. The most strategic was Carthage in Northwest Africa, which was southeast of Sardinia and necessary for the transport of silver and tin from Iberia and Northern Europe. However, the Phoenicians were not always a commercial juggernaut, especially when needing to contend with more powerful neighbors.

Before the Bronze Age Collapse cleared the way for them to become powerful, the Phoenicians mainly traded with the Greeks. At this point in time, the Greeks had established a desirable civilization with numerous city-states and ports dotting the small islands throughout the Mediterranean. The Phoenicians traded wood, slaves, glass, and a powdered dye called Tyrian purple. Artisans made Tyrian purple from the crushed shells of a specific snail that lived in the seas, and it was used by elite officials to color their garments and showcase their status with a single glance. Purple was the rarest color in the ancient world, and it was almost impossible to make, earning the shade a desirable location in the color wheel.

Over time, the Greeks trusted the Phoenicians more. They released some of their hold as trading and colonizing spread across the Mediterranean Sea until the sea split into two halves, with the Phoenicians dominating the south and the Greeks controlling the north. Eventually, this situation would turn on its head, with the Greeks maintaining the east while the Phoenicians settled in the west following the Sicilian Wars.

After the Bronze Age Collapse laid waste to many of the nearby civilizations, the Phoenicians emerged as a major naval and trading power around 1200 BCE. This time, they controlled the immensely desirable Tyrian purple dye, having discovered it could be derived from the hypobranchial gland of the murex sea snail. With this knowledge and a seemingly limitless supply of snails from the coasts they controlled, the Phoenicians were able to establish a massive trade center in Sarepta, a city in modern-day Lebanon. They relied upon the murex snail so much that the Phoenicians eventually caused its local extinction out of greed for the beautiful luxury it provided. Before doing so, the Phoenicians made the snail and its dye the center of their trading empire and even managed to establish a second production center in the city of Mogador, whose ruins lay in contemporary Morocco. Besides dye, glass was another influential export of the Phoenicians because of the difficulty in making glass plates, jars, and beads.

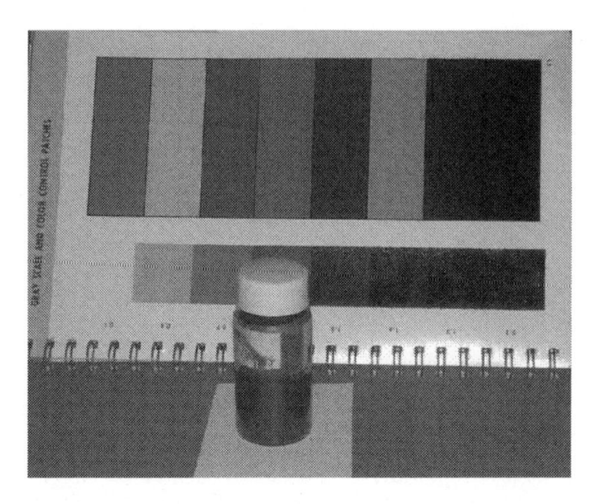

A Major Component of Tyrian Purple Dye

The Phoenicians did not just content themselves with providing non-consumable luxury goods. They were also excellent at filling in gaps in the inventories of other civilizations, especially nearby Egypt. Following the Bronze Age Collapse, the Egyptians struggled to regain their footing in the ancient world, a situation not helped by years of tumultuous dynastic rule. One thing the Egyptians especially lacked when it came to luxuries was wine.

Grapevines could not grow in Egypt, but the Phoenicians possessed ample coastal landscapes to grow massive vineyards capable of producing rich wine. Barrels tended to be shipped to South Lebanon and Sarepta, where the wine would then be stored in handmade pots and sold to Egypt in exchange for Nubian gold. Historians possess a wealth of knowledge about these transactions thanks to vividly documented shipwrecks that were discovered in 1997 about thirty miles west of Ascalon, known as Ashkelon today. By all accounts, the Egyptians were one of the largest consumers of imported wine and provided much of the gold that went into making Phoenician jewelry for men and women.

At the same time, the Phoenicians had discovered that the Egyptians also lacked lumber since their land was primarily desert and flood plains around the Nile River. So, sailors and merchants started to bring massive cedar logs from the mountains of Lebanon down to

Egypt and exchanged them for even more gold, linen, papyrus, and even cowhide. One well-documented transaction occurred sometime between 1075 BCE and 1060 BCE. An Egyptian envoy called Wen-Amon arrived in Phoenicia and bought seven humongous cedar logs for the inordinate sum of "4 crocks and 1 kak-men of gold; 5 silver jugs; 10 garments of royal linen; 10 kherd of good linen from Upper Egypt; 500 rolls of finished papyrus; 500 cows' hides; 500 ropes; 20 bags of lentils, and 30 baskets of fish."[11] Wen-Amon carried the goods back to Egypt by boat and was thought to have secured a great deal for his seven logs, which could be turned around and sold for an even higher sum at home.

However, the path to becoming the most powerful merchants on the Mediterranean would take time. Before they became renowned traders, archaeological evidence indicates that the early Phoenician economy relied heavily on agriculture and animal husbandry. The original Phoenicians inherited this knowledge from their predecessors in the Levant and were thus able to use the temperate climate of their position on the Mediterranean Sea to produce vast staple crops of wheat and barley. These foodstuffs could be used to support a massive and often widespread population, but the extras were also valuable trade goods that could be transferred to partners in Egypt or farther to the east.

The flourishing agricultural economies of the Phoenicians relied on profitable crops like wheat, but they would eventually branch out thanks to technological developments like systems of irrigation and durable plows pulled by oxen rather than human muscle. By 1200 BCE, artifacts indicate agriculture allowed Phoenicia to become so prosperous that members of the population could engage in other pursuits, leading to burgeoning maritime economies on the banks of the Mediterranean. These economies would eventually translate to settlements and colonies throughout the Mediterranean as

---

11 Markoe, Glenn E. (2000). *Peoples of the Past: Phoenicians*. Berkeley, CA: University of California Press, p. 103.

Phoenician maritime prowess allowed the civilization to outsail its competition and lay claim to advantageous locations.

The sea became the integral component of the entire Phoenician economy, with two primary trade goods emerging from its briny depths: A variety of palatable fish and the snails necessary to make the rare purple dye. The shipbuilding industry further flourished and was a necessary component of the economy that was bolstered by the water. To gain the wood necessary for shipbuilding, the Phoenicians logged the nearby forests for their massive cedar trees and dragged the trunks to the coast for shaping. When possible, the Phoenicians avoided buying wood from other civilizations.

Unfortunately, as is the case for most situations concerning the Phoenicians, archaeologists and historians struggle with a lack of direct evidence of trading customs and practices. Most of what is known about trading partners and goods come from the records of friendly civilizations whose tablets explain what the Phoenicians brought with them, who they preferred to conduct business with, and what prices their goods would fetch in local and foreign markets. One benefit of these tablets is that they provide excellent economic information since merchants rarely lied about their transactions, but it comes with the unfortunate lack of a Phoenician perspective on trade.

What historians do understand is that the Phoenicians relied upon soft power, or the political power of their commerce and culture to influence other civilizations and avoid warfare when possible. While their navy was powerful, Phoenicia avoided conflict because their culture, in general, focused on the acquisition of wealth to prosper. By the 12th century BCE, the Phoenicians possessed a mixed economy that had incorporated agricultural, industrial, and commercial sectors with excellent results.

Out of these three sectors, the two most important were agriculture and commerce. Besides being well known for their trade and luxury goods, the Phoenicians manufactured an impressive amount of wine that was coveted throughout the Mediterranean because of its excellent flavor and quality. If any sommeliers existed in ancient times, they no doubt would have been able to identify a Phoenician cabernet from a mile away.

For the purposes of discussing their economy, it is best to divide subjects by whether they functioned primarily as agriculture or commerce. While there was some industry, it mostly focused on shipbuilding.

The Agricultural Sector

The Phoenicians relied on agriculture to feed a growing population that consumed more than it produced when it came to food. Cereal crops and viticulture (wine-growing) were the most significant, but Phoenicia also had its own vegetables and domesticated animals reserved for local use. Up first in this discussion are the cereal grains, which refers to plants like barley and wheat that could be used to make "cereals," or a type of gruel.

Agriculture and husbandry formed the majority of the Phoenician economy, even though so many associate the civilization with trading. Most of the cereal crops grown went to the peasants who cultivated them and who needed the calories to survive. There is evidence that most Phoenician farmers used the crops to pay their taxes. These grains would be transported to a noble's stronghold, where the food would then be kept for personal use or sold to merchants. Since the economy was a mixture of rural and urban, many wealthier landowners paid laborers with food in addition to some money. Similar to the ancient Babylonians, there is evidence to indicate that the amount of food a laborer received was proportionate to gender, age, and overall size. So, a young man received almost twice as much as an elderly woman.

Agricultural cultivation was not a simple process. Because the Phoenicians were on the seacoast, frequent freshwater shortages combined with the salinity of the soil meant farmers needed to be knowledgeable about irrigation to create water reserves. The major city-states grew around arable hinterlands that formed miniature breadbaskets, and they took advantage of irrigation systems to develop rudimentary public sewer systems to keep the cities relatively healthy and clean. The technology of irrigation was also used to develop cisterns and create a network that supplied fresh water to the cities for merchants and laborers. Archaeological investigations revealed that the Phoenicians "cultivated the lower slopes of the Lebanese mountains," which increased the amount of available crop space and eased the entire process of irrigation overall.[12]

Despite extensive cultivation, Phoenicia had a grain deficit. The population grew steadily from the Iron Age onward, and the rocky, arid terrain made it difficult to maintain large fields of cereal grains. So, the Phoenicians had a tendency to grow barley whenever possible, even if it meant tending to small patches of crops. Barley would be gathered and stored in silos to preserve the grains, and it was preferred to growing wheat because it was better at resisting the salinity of the air. To supplement their food, almost everyone grew their own fruits and vegetables to round out their diet and reduce the deficit.

While cereal grain agriculture was essential for survival, the Phoenicians reinforced their agricultural sector by engaging in extensive viticulture. Viticulture is a branch of horticulture that focuses on growing grapes for wine. Unlike cereal grains, which required tons of fresh water and open space that the terrain lacked, Phoenicia was actually perfectly suited for the growing of grapes. It was sunny, rocky, and remained warm throughout the year, allowing vines to grow and supply the Phoenicians with an impressive amount of wine that they could then trade for more grain to battle the deficit. Not surprisingly, the fresh grapes themselves were also desired and could be bought and sold for high prices on the market.

[12] Woolmer, *Ancient Phoenicia*, p. 71.

Mediterranean Red Grapes

A similar product was the olive. Olives were a staple of the Mediterranean diet, and the Phoenicians could cultivate strong olive trees and press the fruits into oil that would be preserved, sold, or used for religious rituals. Like grapes, fresh olives were also prized and bought by civilizations like the Egyptians, who wanted to eat them fresh. Authors like Mark Woolmer, a PhD professor of ancient history, claim olives not only demonstrated political stability, but they were also important because they grew well and matured at different times than cereal grains, meaning manpower was available to harvest both.

A Mediterranean Olive Tree

Wine and olive oil thus enjoyed a coveted position in the Phoenician economy and became tools of trade throughout the ancient world. In

1999, archaeologists discovered two sunken merchant vessels that, when explored, revealed a series of amphorae sealed with pinewood discs. The holds were full of these vessels and appeared to have been ships dedicated to the transport of wine and oil. Not all of it was traded, of course, as members of the local population also enjoyed the fruits of their labors—literally. One of the only known Phoenician philosophers, a man named Zeno, was believed to be so fond of wine that he died from an alcoholic dose from consuming too much in a single sitting.[13]

Besides crops, Phoenicia also engaged in animal husbandry, particularly livestock. However, they also domesticated other animals to suit their purposes. Cattle were the most popular animals because of its tasty beef and ability to produce milk, but donkeys come in a close second. While cattle were eaten, the donkeys were necessary to transport goods across the rocky terrain of modern-day Lebanon. Sheep were great to possess for wool, and goats were essential for milk. Surprisingly, sheep and goats were perhaps the first animals domesticated, and they appeared to be called "small cattle" in the Phoenician language. They were kept in large flocks rather than on small farms. Most flocks were controlled by the state, regional temples, or wealthy landowners who had the means to allow for grazing.

Pastoralism was the name of the game, although most shepherds were hired hands. Because sheep and goat theft were serious crimes, any animals killed while under the watch of a hired hand needed to be presented to the owner as proof that they didn't steal it. The wool went to make clothing, and goat's milk made delicious cheese and yogurt for consumption.

Besides the shepherds, flocks were protected by domesticated dogs. The dog was the primary Phoenician domestic animal and played a serious role in animal protection from local wildlife. Historians have

[13] Some historians speculate that texts could also be referring to liver failure after lifelong consumption, but the rhetoric is unclear.

traced two breeds to the Phoenicians: a large greyhound and a breed that no longer exists but was as tall and strong as a modern Mastiff or Great Dane. There is some evidence that domesticated dogs could be used as war animals and were most likely not traded with other civilizations. The same could not be said for ducks, chickens, and geese, which were popular fowl.

Finally, the Phoenicians stood out for their beekeeping. Honey served as the primary source of sugar for the population, and the ability to tend to bees was a prized skill. Hive beekeeping possesses a history that stretches over thousands of years, so it should be no surprise that honey was popular at this time. In addition to this amber foodstuff, beekeepers also cultivated and used beeswax, which created a watertight sealant and could be used for medicinal purposes. Now that was a sweet deal.

The Commercial Sector

The Phoenicians were merchants first and foremost, and they engaged in interregional trade on an unprecedented scale. However, despite being extensive traders, a trait that stands out about their practices was how they did not implement the minting of national coinage until the middle of the 5th century BCE. Historians trace this failure to adopt coinage to Phoenicia's history of colonization, especially when the civilization became the vassal of the Persians. It was easier to trade with a wide variety of partners while using a system of barter and exchange, and the Persians themselves used an exchange system that did not require coin money.

Eventually, coinage seeped into Phoenicia following the influx of Greek traders that arrived in the Phoenician city-states following the Persian Wars. Greece was one of the first civilizations to mint its own currency, and city-states like Sidon and Tyre followed suit to keep up with the commercial practice. The result was Phoenicia adopting coin money but also having a system where each city-state demonstrated its autonomy by producing its own coinage.[14]

A Carthaginian Shekel, c. 237-227 BCE

The Phoenician currency drew upon themes and ideas present in their Greek counterparts, including the depiction of the current ruler or a favored deity on the front and some sort of national symbol on the back. The coin from the city-state of Carthage above has the face of the god Melqart, their preferred deity, as well as a war elephant, a staple of the North African province. Locations like Sidon, Byblos, and Arwad followed suit, choosing to depict a galley (a type of ship) on their currency.

Because the coins were developed while the Phoenicians struggled under Persian rule, gold was not used. This is because the default coin was the gold Persian shekel, and the rare metal went to the minting of those. Instead, the Phoenicians made a number of silver coins and then eventually incorporated bronze for smaller denominations that could be used by the average citizen. Like any

[14] Interesting Fact: Many coins do not belong to institutions like museums and are regularly bought and sold online as intriguing artifacts or prized possessions for coin collectors. Although the money is no longer in circulation, the coins remain valuable today.

other currency, it took several years for Phoenician money to become widespread.

As merchants, the Phoenician traders remained abreast of the various intricacies of the commercial sector. While they continued to trade the agricultural goods produced in the hinterlands, they also strove to work as moneylenders and needed to navigate a unique position in society. All merchants operated under the auspiciousness of the local monarchy or nobility, and they were expected to engage in a system of gift-giving, exchange, and regular trade. This system was difficult to navigate and necessitated that the merchants adopt a diplomatic role in how they conducted business.

Diplomacy and commerce became intertwined around the 14th century BCE when traders "not only took part in public administration but [were] entrusted by the state with organizing commercial agencies and with buying and selling in the capacity of envoy to the king."[15] This was a holdover from the ancient period, where members of the royal house tended to do all of the trading for the region. By the 8th century BCE, the merchants were able to break away from the old system and develop their own mercantile caste or class, which allowed private families and individuals to accrue wealth for their own purposes.

These merchants enjoyed social status and prestige that set them apart from regular nobles and the common folk. A Phoenician trader was a qualified professional and specialist; they were well educated and often became a part of the extended royal family through marriage and politics. Their skills were in high demand, and most could read, write, and do calculations to maintain their vast networks. Moneylending boomed, and by the seventh and sixth centuries BCE, historians see patterns that indicate the merchants started to form their own "houses" or networks that are reminiscent of the medieval guilds of specialists and craftsmen. Even the royal family started to trade to earn more private wealth and not to help

---

[15] Woolmer, *Ancient Phoenicia,* p. 76.

the city-state. Public and private interests were meshed together, creating a strong economy.

When all is said and done, the agricultural and commercial sectors of the Phoenician economy would not have thrived without the Mediterranean Sea. From their position on the coast, the Phoenicians were posed to exert an immense amount of influence if they could get their goods across the briny deep. To do so, they needed the best ships available that could transport items but also resist and defeat pirates: They needed a merchant navy.

Sailing with a Merchant Navy

In modern culture, the Phoenicians are the most well known for their formidable navy. Shipbuilding was done primarily in Byblos, and the completed vessels could be transported to other locations via waterways. Trading could be done on galleys, where fifty pairs of muscular sailors would row when the wind and waves could not be relied upon. The front bow could be used to ram pirates and triremes when needed, and sailors would fire arrows at oncoming vessels.

Because the Phoenicians wrote on papyrus and lack an abundance of preserved records, modern historians and archaeologists have used shipwrecks to reconstruct the templates of the vessels as well as the more common cargo. The Phoenicians were highly prized for their goods and managed to avoid the majority of military excursions, but they were often susceptible to piracy. Many people were interested in their gold and silver ingots, olive oil, wine, purple dyes, and cedar lumber.

According to archaeologists, there were three different types of ships. Each one was shallow-keeled to be able to traverse the docks and bays of the city-states. The warships were biremes, which had two long rows of oars. The front included a ram, which could be accessed across the wide deck. The second type of ship was also a bireme but had a wide hull capable of storing cargo. The sides of the deck were also high and reinforced so cargo could be stored on top as well. These trading ships often traveled in groups of between twenty and fifty at a time and would be surrounded by warships.

Finally, there was a much smaller trading vessel that could be used for short trips. This one possessed a single bank of oars and often had a horse's head at the bow for decoration and potential religious protection. These boats were not used often; archaeologists think it might have been used for fishing or minor excursions along the coast.

Because of their role as ancient mariners, the Phoenicians lacked navigational devices like the compass. Instead, they relied upon their knowledge of natural features on the coastline and the stars. Historians believe the most important constellation was Ursa Minor. The North Star was essential for navigation and keeping track of the cardinal directions. Up until recently, because of their reliance on the coastline to mark their routes, most historians believe the Phoenicians stuck to the shallows and only sailed during the daytime, weighing anchor at night and waiting for the morning before moving again. Recently, this view has been challenged. In fact, it could have actually been more dangerous for the Phoenicians to stick closer to the coastlines. The sailors would be subjected to more hazards like rocks and shallows there, which could damage their vessels and result in shipwrecks.

The average Phoenician ship was capable of moving at a speed of six miles per hour. In order to get from the Levant to a colony on the Iberian Peninsula, it would take travelers almost ninety days, which would be almost the entire sailing season. The crew would have to wait until the next year to make the voyage back.

Besides this information, it is difficult for historians to distinguish other concrete facts. The routes favored by the Phoenicians are a subject of hot debate, with scholars at one another's throats to determine which ones are true. While there are surviving shipwrecks, the natural currents of the sea would have displaced them by many miles. However, it is known that brave navigators accomplished some unusual feats, including an attempt to sail around the African continent and making it to the Indian Ocean to find new goods to trade.

Chapter 9 – Language and Alphabet

Although the Phoenicians were Canaanites, they developed their own unique language that morphed over time from the traditional Semitic Canaanite to something called Phoenician, or *Put* in ancient Egyptian documents. This language would be a part of the Canaanite subgroup of the Northwest Semitic languages because of its similar grammatical structure and roots to traditional Canaanite, but it managed to distinguish itself by being codified, ascribed a clear alphabet, and was somewhat standardized by the upper echelons of society. Other members of the same language family are Hebrew, Edomite, Moabite, and Ammonite. All developed in societies that began as Canaanites and then formed their own separate cultures.

Because the Phoenicians possessed an extensive network of city-states, the language was spoken around the coastal Mediterranean region. Some of the areas where it could have been heard include the region of Greater Syria and Anatolia, which encompasses modern-day countries like Lebanon, Israel/Palestine, Syria, Turkey, and Cyprus. It could also be heard in colonized areas like present-day

Morocco, Algeria, Libya, Tunisia, Sicily, Sardinia, Corsica, Malta, the Balearic Islands, and most of southern Spain. While it functioned as a common language, meaning lower-class people would speak it daily, it was also taught and learned as a prestige language among the Greeks and Egyptians for more effective trade between civilizations.

Although they were preceded by other Canaanite societies, the Phoenicians were the first state-level society that used the Semitic alphabet on a widespread level to teach and understand the language. The accompanying alphabet is also the oldest verified consonantal alphabet in the world, meaning it is the first alphabet with characters that represent consonants that has evidence to support its age. Most archaeologists consider the language to be "Proto-Canaanite" until 1050 BCE when remaining artifacts start to bear a more distinct language. Scholars think the Phoenician phonetic alphabet might actually be a partial ancestor to almost every current contemporary alphabet in existence, with exceptions made for distance.

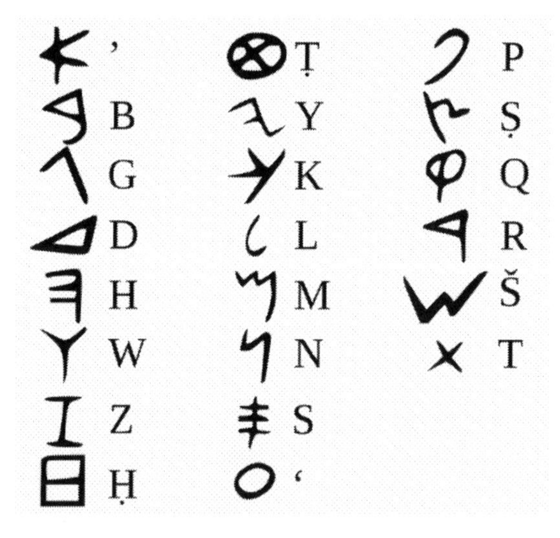

The Early Phoenician Alphabet

Phoenician holds a unique place from a linguistic perspective simply because scholars struggle to determine just how different it was from Canaanite, which is not well understood. Texts and artifacts do not indicate whether Phoenician possessed slight differences, was superficial in its development, or if it was a truly complex and unique language. Whatever the case may be, their alphabet would be adopted around the Mediterranean because of its importance to trade. An example of this in more contemporary times is how many countries and cultures learned to speak English to conduct business with the East India Company and other modern businesses on a regular basis.

The Phoenician alphabet rapidly spread to the Greeks, who used it as a template to create their Greek alphabet. The Greek alphabet, in turn, spread to the Etruscans and Romans, with the latter creating the Latin alphabet. Several cultures in Northern Africa also adopted it, including the peoples in the region of Morocco. At some point, the future Carthaginian civilization would colonize much of the Western Mediterranean and spread Phoenician as well, where it would become the distinct Punic language. Punic died out well after Phoenician since it survived until the 5th century CE. The Romans would colonize former Carthaginian areas, spreading Latin instead.

The Alphabet

After decades of using the Proto-Canaanite script, the Phoenicians eventually developed their own alphabet to record their language. This script is called an abjad, meaning it focuses on the use of consonants rather than syllables when it comes to written characters. Many historians believe Phoenician was essential because it formed the basis of the later Greek alphabet, which, in turn, influenced the Latin alphabet. As mentioned earlier, the Carthaginians also continued to use the alphabet after the Phoenicians themselves disappeared, resulting in the unique Punic form of the script.

The Punic writing was slightly different from the original Phoenician one. While the Phoenicians wrote in large block letters, the Carthaginians developed a more cursive shape to their letters. Around the 3rd century BCE, the Punic alphabet featured the presence of vowels, which had been largely ignored by the

Phoenicians. Final vowels also got more attention, and they sometimes have characters like an aleph or an ayin marking them. The letter aleph is a character derived from the appearance of an ox's head, while an ayin is a symbol in some alphabets that meant the person needed to pronounce a character with a pharyngeal fricative. In other words, both symbols changed traditional pronunciations and placed emphasis on the final vowel.

The Punic alphabet formed perhaps the most lasting imprint of the original Phoenician, and it continued to grow and evolve for centuries. Around the time of the Second Punic War, the script became even more cursive in appearance. This would evolve into Neo-Punic, which was more conservative than the original Punic. By conservative, this meant it had fewer details, which was fitting since it emerged after the destruction of Carthage by Rome around 146 BCE. Neo-Punic was more organized and standardized than regular Punic and the original Phoenician alphabet because it had specific "consonantal letters" to distinguish between vowel sounds. This was different because the original Phoenician did not mark vowels, while Punic had a couple of ways to write a single vowel sound, which could be confusing for individuals who tried to read the script, even with context.

With all of this in mind, what made Phoenician distinct? It was certainly different from other abjads at the time, like Aramaic, Arabic, and Biblical Hebrew. In the written form, long vowels were not expressed and were not recorded even if they came from diphthongs. This meant anyone reading a Phoenician document would need to know how words were pronounced and which consonants were involved; otherwise, the writing would be unintelligible. It wasn't until Phoenician evolved into Punic that scribes and writers started to use symbols to mark final and long vowels, giving modern scholars a fighting chance when it comes to deciphering the language. Linguists and historians know the most about Phoenician vowels from these Punic inscriptions, which were frequently translated into Greek and other languages.

Surviving Examples

Phoenician, combined with Punic, has approximately 10,000 surviving inscriptions around the Mediterranean that can be examined by historical linguists to piece together the language. These inscriptions can be supplemented with the glossaries of books written in other ancient languages like Greek, Latin, and Arabic, which explain a couple of the words and offer rough translations. Although the Phoenicians appeared to be prolific writers because of the nature of their trading civilization, few sources have survived, meaning it is difficult for contemporary audiences to fully understand the Phoenician language and alphabet.

When it was time to write, the Phoenicians did not choose to use mud or clay tablets and avoided inscriptions in stone unless they were meant for a coffin or tomb. Instead, the traders and scribes used papyrus or parchment sheets that would have degraded quickly, making it almost impossible for examples to survive. This means there are no histories or trading records since all of the papyrus and leather rotted or molded away in the damp conditions surrounding the Phoenician city-states by the sea. This jewel of a civilization quite literally degraded in the earth even though the Phoenicians were responsible for spreading literacy and the ability to write among numerous social classes and members of the population. The only physical sources available, besides those in tombs, are a couple of letters and notes on broken pottery, three fragments of papyri, and some monumental inscriptions carved in stone.

Such a lack of information is daunting and disappointing, considering the Phoenicians and Carthaginians seemed to write entire books, as alluded to by Roman authors like Sallust. Only a few volumes survived thanks to the rare translation into Latin or the preservation of a couple of snippets in Roman plays— for some examples, see Mago's treatise or Plautus' plays. Phoenician remained such a mystery that it was not until the Cippi of Melqart was discovered in Malta in 1694 CE that a French scholar, Jean-Jacques Barthelemy, was able to decipher and reconstruct the Punic alphabet around 1764. The Cippi of Melqart was a bilingual inscription in ancient Greek and Punic.

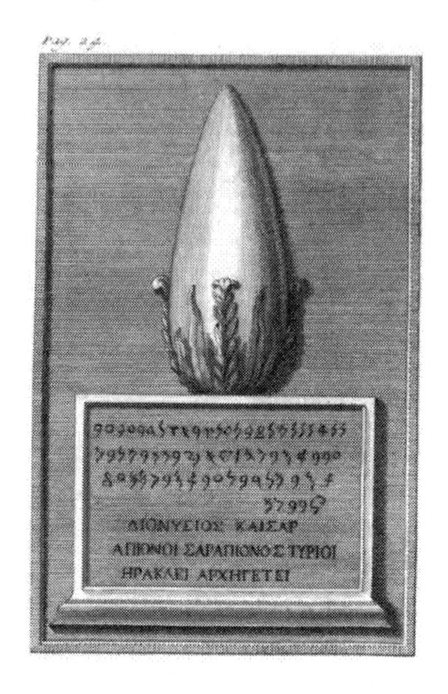

Guyot de Marne's Drawing of the Cippi of Melqart, c. 1760

Besides the Cippi of Melqart, there are few significant surviving inscriptions of Phoenician. Some of the most well-known and influential examples are the Ahiram sarcophagus, the Nora Stone, the Pyrgi Tablets, and the Temple of Eshmun.

The Ahiram sarcophagus is the sarcophagus of a Phoenician king of Byblos who ruled c. 1000 BCE. The stone resting place was uncovered in 1923 by excavator Pierre Montet in tomb V of the royal necropolis of Byblos. The sarcophagus bears magnificent bas-reliefs and has 38 words written on it in an old Phoenician dialect from the region of Byblos. It currently resides in Lebanon and provides an excellent source of the original Phoenician alphabet and some of the common imagery and artwork from the time. The translation of the 38 words appears to say the following (according to the most recent work done by ancient linguists):

> A coffin made it [Pil]sibaal, son of Ahirom, king of Byblos, for Ahirom, his father, lo, thus he put him in seclusion. Now,

if a king among kings and a governor among governors and a commander of an army should come up against Byblos; and when he then uncovers this coffin – (then:) may strip off the sceptre of his judiciary, may be overturned the throne of his kingdom, and peace and quiet may flee from Byblos. And as for him, one should cancel his registration concerning the libation tube of the memorial sacrifice.[16]

The Sarcophagus of Ahiram

The Nora Stone, also called the Nora Inscription, is a stone stele discovered on the southern coast of Sardinia in 1773 CE. The stele comes from the late 9th or early 8th century BCE and is one of the oldest inscriptions found around Sardinia. The inscriptions have been difficult to translate, but scholars believe they convey the message that a general won an influential battle in the region and erected the stele as a monument to his victory. Others give the writing a more religious connotation.

The Pyrgi Tablets are a couple of bilingual tablets that present inscriptions in Etruscan and Phoenician. These have been dated to 500 BCE and were discovered in 1964 CE. Linguists were actually able to decipher more Etruscan from the slightly better-known Phoenician from these tablets. They were found during the excavation of a sanctuary of ancient Pyrgi on the Tyrrhenian coast of

[16] Reinhard G. Lehmann: Die Inschrift(en) des Ahirom-Sarkophags und die Schachtinschrift des Grabes V in Jbeil (Byblos), 2005, p. 38

Italy, explaining the presence of Etruscan. The writing appears to be a dedication to the Phoenician goddess ‘Ashtaret.

Finally, there is the important Temple of Eshmun. This temple was dedicated to the deity Eshmun, who was a Phoenician god of healing. The temple is located in the northeast of Sidon in Lebanon, and it appeared to be occupied between the 7th century BCE and the 8th century CE. After the Phoenicians, other cultures, like the native Sidonians and Arabs, occupied the temple. This temple serves as a great example of Phoenician architecture, but it also features several influential inscriptions that have allowed scholars to decipher a little of the Phoenician language and alphabet. Most of the inscriptions were found during the 20th century CE and include examples like the following:

As far as people have been able to tell, this particular inscription is funerary writing from the 4th century BCE for King Bodashtart of Sidon.

Chapter 10 – Religion

Historians do not possess many primary sources for the Phoenician religion and must instead rely on the biased and often negative reports given by neighboring civilizations like the Jewish and the later Christians in Israel, Babylon, and Egypt. Around this point in time, a religious schism emerged between those who practiced polytheistic religions, or religions that have multiple deities, and populations that embraced monotheism, or the belief in a single god. The early Jewish and Christians, particularly in Israel and nearby areas, wrote negatively about rival civilizations, and their works have been well preserved due to the continuing popularity of the Abrahamic religions in modern society.

Direct information about Phoenician religion only comes from the inscriptions left on sarcophagi and in tombs, but this often isn't enough to counter the accusations of base and monstrous behaviors such as ritual human sacrifice, which was common in almost every religion of the Bronze Age and early Iron Age. Inscriptions reveal the Phoenicians were deeply polytheistic and inherited the Mesopotamian pantheon from their Canaanite ancestors, which stressed the single creator god of Ba'al and a massive pantheon of other deities.

Bronze Figurine of Ba'al, c. 14th-12th century BCE

However, it is difficult to describe a Phoenician pantheon, as religion was divided between the city-states. Each one adopted or stressed a different patron deity who was thought to watch over the region. This figure, whether they created the universe or not, received the most libations and prayers and was seen as the most significant or influential deity in the Phoenician pantheon, as well as the religion as a whole, within a set region. So, while one city might worship Ba'al more than the others, another might think Astarte was the most significant.

While Ba'al had tantamount importance before c. 1200 BCE, this all changed with a religious upheaval that saw the Phoenicians embracing lesser-known goddesses like Astarte and creating new deities like Melqart, Eshmun, and Reshef. Besides these gods and goddesses, the Phoenicians were also considerably influenced by the pantheons of the Egyptians, Hurrians, Mesopotamians, and others, so the total number of deities worshiped by the Phoenicians came from a hodgepodge of multiple cultures.

The Practices of the Cult

When contemporary audiences hear the phrase "cult," they often think of a secretive, evil religion or leaders like Jim Jones, who orchestrated mass suicides among fanatic followers. For ancient religions, the term cult refers to the practices of the followers of a particular deity. For example, there was the cult of Melqart and the cult of Ba'al. These practices varied between locations but also shared some significant central similarities, especially in relation to the calendar.

The Phoenician cultic calendar was inspired by the agricultural one, with sacrifices correlating with planting, harvesting, and other significant events. For example, libations were often poured when the first fruits appeared and when dairy products became available after the new year. The fertility of the earth was connected with the fertility of humans, and the movements of the sun and the moon affected the calendar as well, with sacrifices performed for solstices, eclipses, and even new or full moons. The moon, in particular, held special importance for the Phoenicians because they believed the moon died during each cycle and was then resurrected.

Cult rituals and rites took place near nature, with religious officials venturing out to mountains, near rivers, in forests, or beyond the city walls to sacred sites. Many practices mirrored religious legends, including reenacting the burning and resurrection of Melqart. However, the accusations of regular sacrifices draw the most ire from neighboring civilizations and even modern audiences. Although human sacrifice is up for debate, the faithful did kill lambs, sheep, and similar animals on a regular basis. These were often left with vegetables and other foodstuffs.

When it comes to human sacrifice, the bodies of stillborn infants were discovered in sacred sites, along with some human bones. Historians fall into two camps about the infants. They were either venerated in some way by the culture and were offered to the deities because they were born dead, or they might have been born healthy before being smothered or strangled as a sacrifice. Surviving inscriptions that do reference these practices seem to indicate that human sacrifice did occur, but it was often of adults and only performed during times of great trouble, such as a famine.

Besides animals, food, and the occasional human, the faithful tended to give the gods and goddesses votives or similar items made for a religious purpose and dedicated to the deities. Some examples include small bronze statues, bowls, dishes, jars of wine and olive oil, and sometimes ivory or stone sculptures. These could be given in individual ceremonies but were often showered *en masse* upon a deity during a feast or festival. Artifacts depict religious officials and female adherents or dancers bringing votives to sacred sites, and texts mention that there were feasts, dances, and other rituals performed on holy days. Women could be religious officials to an extent, but they were limited in their freedoms.

In the cities, ritual feasts held special importance and occurred at a *marzeh*, or "place of reunion." Each place developed as a location where friends and kin could gather and celebrate while honoring deceased ancestors. Over time, powerful *marzeh* started to influence the political and commercial lives of locations like Tyre, demonstrating how religion often blended into politics and the overall social structure.

Finally, divination and belomancy played a role in the outcomes of political decisions and personal lives. Diviners were specially trained religious officials who would search for signs or symbols in nature and interpret them to learn the outcome of future events. Belomancy was a sub-category of this practice that focused on examining the flight of arrows. Omens and portents could be found anywhere, including dreams and the entrails of animals. The result was a complex world of rituals, superstition, and political relationships that characterized the Phoenicians for over one thousand years.

Astarte

Astarte was a marginalized goddess in the Near Eastern pantheon that was brought to new importance by the Phoenicians, who worshiped her heavily in Tyre, Sidon, and Byblos. She was associated with fertility, sexuality, and war, and she possessed numerous animal motifs, including the lion, sphinx, and dove. She was further depicted with the stars and the moon, with the crescent moon being her most common symbol. She was the virgin daughter of a sky god and was perhaps the most commonly depicted female deity throughout the Phoenician territories. A marble statue of her is depicted below.

Melqart

Melqart was the chief deity of Tyre and was believed to be the progenitor of the Tyrian royal family. His worship spread from Lebanon to Spain, and he was associated with Heracles by the Greeks and Hercules with the Romans. The majority of the archaeological evidence about him comes from temples located in North Africa and the Iberian Peninsula, but it tends to be limited to statuary and inscriptions on sarcophagi.

Melqart was associated with the sea, commerce, nobility, royalty, and colonization. He was the central focus of a festival of resurrection during a month that encompassed modern-day February and March, during which an effigy of him was burnt and then resurrected. This gives him associations with fire as well, and he was further believed to be the founder of the murex purple dye for which the Phoenicians became well known.

Special temples were dedicated to Melqart, and a sacred precinct functioned as the treasury of the city. Women, foreigners, and pigs—of all things—were not allowed to enter the precinct, even during rituals and festivals. All three groups were seen as unworthy or unclean in some fashion. Human sacrifices appear to have been given to him during times of strife and stress. Over time, as Phoenician influence waned and the Greeks and Romans started to become more powerful, Melqart became associated with Hercules (Heracles for the Greeks) and the twelve labors. Historians debate whether this has connotations to wrestling or if the twelve labors symbolized how the Phoenicians ventured all around the Mediterranean Sea.

Eshmun

Eshmun was the god of healing and the chief deity of Sidon. Unlike several other gods, he was worshiped in multiple city-states because of his benign pantheon. Little is known of him except that he had multiple dedicated temples and inscriptions that depict him wielding a staff with two snakes that could have been the inspiration for several influential contemporary symbols. He is associated with the Greek god Apollo, although some compare him to Apollo's son, Asclepius.

The Afterlife

For the Phoenicians, death appeared to be a genuine supernatural being that represented the chaos of the universe. After having lost a dispute with the other deities, Death, known as the god Mot to the Phoenicians, was punished and had its power limited to only control humans. Although Death was not worshiped like other gods and goddesses, the Phoenicians possessed a complex relationship with Death, especially in funerary rites. Periods of mourning and lamentation were required during a funeral to guarantee safe passage to the afterlife, and people covered themselves in ashes, tore out their hair, wailed, and beat themselves. Pottery and figurines were broken, and a tomb was only sealed with libations and prayers, potentially to Death itself.

When it comes to the afterlife, few sources survive that depict the exact Phoenician beliefs. The religion did not seem to draw much of a distinction between the body and the soul, and historians have been unable to determine whether the Phoenicians believed any life awaited them after death. Bodies were prepped before being left in tombs, often by being wrapped and doused with perfumed oil. Inscriptions over tombs hold warnings about visitors disturbing the eternal sleep of occupants, leading some to believe that the Phoenicians believed people, and their souls by extension, would sleep forever after death.

Chapter 11 – Warfare

The Levantine peoples often warred not only with each other but also with the nearby civilizations in North Africa and across the Mediterranean Sea, including the early ancient Greeks. These wars occurred for a variety of reasons, but the most common justifications were for the attainment of commercial wealth, the control of trade routes, a desire for local natural resources like timber or iron, and boundary disputes. Although the Phoenicians loved the sea, they were no exception to the rule and appeared to have a ground military force as well, though few records survive of battles or encounters. Like the Mesopotamian civilizations, the Phoenician city-states considered war to be a form of divine punishment or retribution.

As far as historians can tell, these city-states were unable to muster large armies because of a lack of extensive territorial resources. While Phoenicia included many city-states across the Mediterranean, they did not have sufficient ground to raise and maintain an army, and they did run on a grain deficit, which made feeding soldiers difficult. Instead of keeping a standing army then, it is likely the Phoenicians would muster a civilian force in times of need and supplement the native troops with mercenaries purchased from nearby Anatolia.

The Army

Without a form of regular training, there was no standardization for the Phoenician soldier. Records indicate men conscripted to fight brought along the dangerous tools of their trade rather than receiving training in more significant weapons like the sword or bow. For example, a hunter who was press-ganged into defending a location like Tyre would arrive and fight using his own ax, bow, or sling. Only if a man didn't have access to implements such as these—for instance, if he was a farmer—would the city government provide borrowed weapons like spears, swords, bows, maces, and small or large shields.

By the 7th century BCE, there is adequate archaeological evidence indicating the full implementation of iron weapons. Spearheads and short swords have been found in poor graves rather than just those of the rich or nobility, and masses of weaponry were discovered in locations like Sardinia. The Phoenicians appeared to make some of their own weapons, but they most likely imported the majority from centers like Anatolia, especially when they purchased the assistance of mercenaries and marauders.

A Phoenician sword varied in length but was most often between 82 and 130 centimeters (between a little over 32 and 51 inches) with a straight blade. The blade was thick and triangular in the center but had tapered edges that ended in clean, sharp ends that could be used for hacking and slashing. The tip was blunt, so piercing was not possible. This indicates a fighting style that did not incorporate thrusting, potentially because enemies most likely wore some version of iron plate mail that could not be pierced easily.

An unfortunate reality for a Phoenician soldier was that he would be well equipped for an offensive campaign but lacked defense. Besides swords, there is evidence of spears and maces being well made with fine iron and sharp tips, but little to no armor has been found. The Phoenicians themselves also rarely depicted their soldiers wearing armor, helmets, boots, gauntlets, or other basic necessities of protecting one's person from harm. This resulted in the deaths of many conscripted citizens. It is theorized that the Anatolian mercenaries were better equipped and were more likely to survive an encounter.

Like other ancient Near Eastern civilizations, the Phoenicians made heavy use of the oriental bow, and by the 1200s BCE, there is significant evidence the composite bow was adopted. Huge numbers of archers and slingers supplemented the infantry, often firing from a distance and attempting to eliminate their enemy counterparts. These older composite bows could be fired with a maximum distance of around 150 to 200 meters. Anything farther required intense strength and skill, and the archers would be unable to track individual targets. The oriental bow design was crucial for rapid-fire, as it could be drawn using several fingers and the archer could hold multiple arrows in hand for quick reloading and fast shots. Because the bow was drawn over the knee, their shots were powerful and covered a great range.

In terms of cavalry, the Phoenicians seem to have implemented the Near Eastern chariot. The Carthaginians, in particular, used over 2,000 models during the Punic Wars. These chariots were made of heavy terracotta and required four horses to function. Teams of three men would ride atop, with one driving, one firing a ranged weapon, and another equipped with a sword for close combat. Sharp blades on the wheel hubs were used to cut through the legs of enemy soldiers who got too close, and a couple of models had similar blades along the back as well. They were formidable weapons and required intensive training, meaning nobles or career soldiers were more likely to use one.

Besides chariots, the Carthaginians also used war elephants. Carthage's propensity for elephants is so well known that it is the first thing people often remember of the city-state, with many recalling how one general, Hannibal Barca, crossed the treacherous Alps with a large elephant force. Even famous TV shows like *The Simpsons* reference the conflict that ensued after Hannibal's forces crossed, and artists from previous centuries were captivated by the idea of transporting the magnificent animals across the sea and into the mountains.

***Hannibal Barca Crossing the Rhône*, by Henri Motte, 1878**

The war elephants were a highly effective force. On the one hand, they formed a source of intimidation against enemy troops, who needed to contend with these large beasts that made thundering trumpet noises, had massive tusks, and could crush a man with their feet. Atop the elephants was another threat, as archers would be walled inside small shelters on the animal's back. These riders had bows and slings, often with ammo tipped in poison, and attempted to kill anyone who got near the elephant's legs.

Bringing elephants onto the battlefield was a dangerous pursuit. Although powerful, a wounded elephant would often turn on its handlers and needed to be killed, at which point the riders were at the mercy of nearby enemy soldiers. However, they intimidated enemy leaders fiercely, including Alexander the Great. When he first encountered the Indian war elephant during his conquest of Mesopotamia in the 4th century BCE, he was so startled that he made a sacrifice to the "God of Fear" (Phobos) the night before the Battle of Gaugamela.

Fortifications, Walls, and Other City Defenses

Because their civilization consisted of powerful city-states, the Phoenicians spent a great deal of time and money fortifying them from sieges and direct assaults. The necessity for walls was strengthened by the fact that each city also consisted of heavy commercial centers with cash, goods, and valuables kept stocked by the merchants in their homes and warehouses. Phoenicia and its territories were always under the threat of attack, and the location of the central city-states didn't help.

While other civilizations like Egypt had the advantage of being south of the majority of the Levant, or Greece who was across the Mediterranean Sea, most Phoenicians lived right in the center of the overland routes that connected the Mediterranean world to the fertile lands of Western Asia. As such, numerous warlords strove to take the territory to control routes of trade and transportation, including Alexander the Great in the 330s BCE.

When they first appeared, walls and other fortifications did not surround the entire city and were instead used to prevent livestock from becoming the prey of wild animals and unscrupulous poachers. Some also served as protection from flash floods, which were capable of wiping away an entire residential sector with immense crushing water. Over time, mudbrick walls gave way to genuine stone variants and became a symbol of wealth and power.

The standard wall consisted of foundations that were partly brick and partly clay. Parapets were made of brick, while stone was used to defend key points. Gates were built into the walls to allow the regular movement of people, and ramparts were necessary to support a large number of archers. When possible, the Phoenicians preferred to retreat to their cities and fire at enemies from afar, which reduced casualties and benefited the population. During the Late Iron Age, the Phoenicians implemented new construction technologies like gypsum cement for fortifications and the implementation of defensive ditches for horses to fall in.

While walls were effective against sieges, they also did lead to overconfidence, and the Phoenicians only enjoyed a brief period of peace before they became the vassals of larger, more powerful civilizations. In particular, the case of Tyre against Alexander the Great demonstrates how putting too much confidence in fortifications can result in an entire city being sieged, burned, and then ransacked. Whether or not this is the best example, though, comes down to whether or not one believes Alexander the Great is a shining example of a regular conqueror.

In the Navy

Although the Phoenicians did engage in ground warfare, they truly shone on the water. The civilization started its pattern of sea exploration on a series of clumsy rafts but eventually built up to hulled vessels based on Assyrian models and the penteconter, a galley that was rowed with fifty pairs of oars. After these developments came an expansion in overseas commerce and the eventual development of the warship, which was independent of the standard merchant vessels but could function as one if needed.

The Phoenician warship advanced significantly from the 8th century to the 5th century BCE. They were propelled by two lines of rowers and featured rams tipped with metallic heads that could be used to crush enemy ships and cause serious hull damage. Archers would line the deck and shoot at enemies as the warship came in proximity to other galleys, and it was necessary to try and break the opponent's oars so they could not row or maneuver normally.

Unlike modern vessels, ancient warships emphasized maneuverability and speed. Phoenician warships featured hollow hulls that ensured each vessel was swift and light, although this did mean hits from an enemy ram could be deadly. Like commercial ships, the standard warship was constructed with hard resin woods, like cypress, oak, and cedar, to better withstand impact. Nonessential interior components could be made of softwood, and the shell was built first. Everything received a waterproof coating, and some warships might have been treated to resist fire as well.

During the Battle of Salamis in 480 BCE, historical records indicate that 300 Phoenician warships were involved in the conflict. These ships carried a total of 30,000 sailors, meaning a single vessel could hold 100 individuals. Many of these men would have spent their time rowing, while others manned sails or shot at enemies.

In about 700 BCE, the Greeks adopted the trireme from the Phoenicians. The trireme had three banks of oars that ensured faster movement, even though the vessel was heavier than the bireme, or a ship with two rows. Relative to the Greek trireme, the Phoenician trireme had a raised deck, used a longer ram, and included amulets or figureheads of protection designed to keep the sailors safe through the supervision of the gods. Near the amulets were apotropaic eyes, which were intended to be a countercharm against misfortune but also as a symbol that would allow the ship to "see" as it sailed.[17]

Relief of a Phoenician Warship, c. 700 BCE

The Phoenician trireme was considered to be the most advanced and powerful ship in the ancient Mediterranean world, with civilizations like the Greeks and Egyptians writing at length about the superiority of Phoenicia's warships and sailors. Because the city-states relied so much on naval warfare, it should not be surprising that they carved a name for themselves on the seas. However, one major reason why the Phoenician ships survived as long as they did was their regular maintenance.

The Phoenicians possessed a unique view of their ships, often considering them living entities that were under the protection of the Cabiri. The Cabiri were chthonic deities who could be appeased through blood sacrifices and who would protect the sailors and others aboard the vessel once they were satisfied.[18] The exact nature of how much the Phoenicians actually sacrificed to these gods is a subject of debate, though. Greek and Roman historians alluded to the practice, but like accusations leveled against the Canaanites, this information needs to be taken with a grain of salt.

One Roman historian, Valerius Maximus, says that the launch of the Carthaginian warships involved a brutal ceremony where prisoners were captured, tied in the water, and then crushed by the hull of a warship so their skulls would shatter and blood would splatter against the wood. The captives' blood was intended to ensure victory and the safe passage of the sailors and soldiers. As Carthage was one of the Phoenician city-states, ancient historians attribute this brutality to the civilization as a whole. However, modern historians believe this is an exaggeration designed to slander an enemy.

[17] Apotropaic magic is a form that is intended to prevent harm and turn away evil influences. The most common form seen in modern Western cultures is the evil eye, designed to stop misfortune from befalling the wearer.

[18] The chthonic deities were subterranean or underworld gods that required blood sacrifices. Deities across multiple religions qualify as chthonic.

Chapter 12 – Artistry in Multiple Mediums

Phoenician art encompasses numerous mediums that evolved over a thousand years, resulting in creative pieces that combined cultural symbols with technological developments. Contemporary audiences are familiar with pieces from the Egyptians, Greeks, and Romans, but in the ancient Mediterranean world, it was the Phoenicians who were considered some of the most skilled artists. Craftsmen and women were lauded for their capabilities, especially when it came to dyes, textiles, and ivory. The monopoly the Phoenicians possessed on the luxurious purple dye meant that Phoenician artists were able to give their work a distinctive color, and their ability to move quickly across the sea meant goods could be transported simply and easily.

Historians and writers like Homer adored the Phoenicians and wrote passages such as:

> …a mixing bowl of silver, richly wrought; six measures it held, and in beauty it was far the goodliest in all the earth, seeing that Sidonians, well skilled in deft handiwork, had

> wrought it cunningly, and men of the Phoenicians brought it over the murky deep, and landed it in harbor…[19]

However, modern artistic communities are less than pleased with the work of the Phoenicians. The chief criticisms of the Phoenicians are that their pieces were ultimately derivative, with motifs, symbols, and imagery heavily borrowed from other cultures and civilizations and then mixed into a hodgepodge stew served to the rest of the Mediterranean. Of glaring significance is that many of the borrowed symbols were misused and placed in situations where they didn't make any sense; instead, they were just used because the appearance was aesthetically pleasing. Some historians argue against this criticism, claiming the combination of multiple elements ultimately shows Phoenician skill and creativity.

Ultimately, whether or not Phoenician art is special or worthy of study remains up to individual preferences. It is difficult to identify characteristics that could be considered defining of the Phoenician collection overall, but Woolmer states it best when he notes, "…the primary characteristic of Phoenician art is its eclecticism."[20] It loved to adopt the styles of Egypt, Assyria, Anatolia, and Syria and translated preexisting symbolism into new mediums. The Phoenicians did so to such a great extent that ancient art historians decided to divide Phoenician artwork into categories based on which civilization the pieces seemed to emulate the most. At present, four exist:

Assyrianizing: This is a style when the Phoenicians copied elements of Assyrian and Hittite culture, usually using imagery like sphinxes, lions, Assyrian seals, and Assyrian fashion. Characteristics of Mesopotamian religion were present as well.

Cypro-Phoenician: This is a set of artworks found only in Cyprus that used solely Assyrian elements instead of combining with

[19] Iliad 23.740
[20] Woolmer, *Ancient Phoenicia*, p. 112.

Egyptian culture, which became common during the broader Mediterranean expansion.

Egyptianizing: Much of Phoenician art is considered to be Egyptianized, or to have copied common Egyptian imagery like sun discs, wingless sphinxes, and Egyptian fashion. It became so popular that Cyprus distinguished itself by clinging to Assyrian culture rather than adopting Egyptian elements.

Syrianizing: The Phoenicians copied Syrian art styles, depicting people in Syrian dress and profile while still retaining Egyptian elements. The main difference between Syrianized Phoenician artwork and regular Syrian work was that the Syrians drew people facing forward with more distinct facial features.

This mixing of styles and symbolism has been known to historians and archaeologists for centuries, with one commenter writing in the New York Times in 1879:

> He entered into other men's labors and made most of his heritage. The Sphinx of Egypt became Asiatic, and its new form was transplanted to Nineveh on the one side and to Greece on the other. The rosettes and other patterns of the Babylonian cylinders were introduced into the handiwork of Phoenicia, and so passed on to the West, while the hero of the ancient Chaldean epic became first the Tyrian Melkarth, and then the Herakles of Hellas.[21]

Most of the information historians possess about Phoenician artwork comes from grave goods, or items that were buried with their owners. These goods were given as signs of an individual's respect toward the deceased or to represent the wealth of the buried, and they could consist of a broad range of objects like bowls, plates, jewelry, small statuettes, scarabs of protection, mirrors, ivory boxes, razors, and terracotta masks. Historians believe funerary art

[21] "Phoenician Art" (PDF). *The New York Times*. 1879-01-05. Retrieved August 22nd, 2019.

constituted a massive portion of artisan work, although many items were made for aesthetic reasons as well.

When examining Phoenician art, scholars must handle the realities of many buildings and papyrus documents being lost to time. While the murals and drawings of other cultures can be examined, the Phoenicians must be analyzed from the position of material objects. The most prevalent types were terracotta masks, metal goods, ivory and stone sculptures, and textiles. While artisans also worked heavily with glass and faience, the Phoenicians preferred to ship glass as a raw material but did keep some to produce jewelry and small votives.

Terracotta

Terracotta objects are clay ceramics with a distinct reddish-brown hue. Unlike other art that was heavily influenced by neighboring civilizations, the terracotta produced by the Phoenicians was intended for domestic use and therefore contained more elements of traditional folk art. Lines were cruder, more exaggerated, and rough. The most commonplace creation was a mask that could be worn for religious purposes. These masks varied, but most possessed dramatic expressions, twisted smiles, and elongated features.

Evidence exists that suggests the masks were painted with vibrant colors after being marked to indicate where the paints would go. Masks were worn by individuals of all ages, including children. Those entering their teenage years and thus coming into adulthood had ceremonious ones to be worn during initiation rituals, rites, and dances. Although early masks were handmade, newer models show signs of being mass-produced from templates.

Besides masks, the Phoenicians also created statuettes of favored gods and goddesses. In one colony, archaeologists discovered hundreds of figurines of a favored goddess that had been crafted using a mold, indicating these statuettes were popular outside of central cities. The masks, on the other hand, were limited to the

Lebanon and Middle Eastern regions and are not often found on other shores of the Mediterranean.

Terracotta objects are divided into three categories: those that were handmade, those spun on a wheel, and those that were made with a mold. In general, handmade offerings are rougher, cruder, and tend to be located in the graves of the poor. These items also are far more likely to be basic goods like pots, cups, and plates than statuettes. Goods made on a wheel are more uniform, while those made in a mold tended to be small votive offerings given to the deities during religious ceremonies. The most common figure discovered is of a woman holding or supporting her breasts, perhaps depicting Astarte. The second is a pregnant woman with her hand on her stomach, symbolizing fertility.

Metalworking

The Phoenicians developed an exceptional reputation for their metalworking capabilities, with metal bowls appearing throughout the Mediterranean region. These bowls featured intricate designs, such as winged sphinxes, and synthesized numerous cultural styles and symbols. Archaeologists date Phoenician metalworking over a span of 800 years, although the best examples emerged between 900 and 700 BCE. Bowls all possessed a circular central medallion with other scenes and designs placed beyond concentric circles that surrounded the center.

Phoenician metal bowls were shallow and primarily depicted Egyptian and Assyrian imagery, with some models even showing an Egyptian pharaoh smiting nearby civilizations. Other common elements were duels, religious scenes, nature, animals, and mythological creatures—the sphinx was, again, a favorite. Copper alloy was the favored metal, but some were made of silver and gold, with personal names inscribed along the inside, potentially revealing the owners of these fine items.

The Phoenicians inherited the knowledge of bronze metalworking from their ancestors in the Levant, and they rapidly adopted ironworking and the skills to work with precious metals. The majority of the bowls produced appear to have a religious purpose, perhaps for making libations due to their shallow nature. Archaeologists theorize that more common dishes would have been made of terracotta or similar hardened clay. An interesting characteristic of many of the bowls, though, is that while they display Egyptian characteristics and symbols, these symbols don't actually make any sense. They were not intended for an Egyptian audience but were most likely shipped as tourist items to cities and civilizations in Europe and Asia.

Other bronze items that were popular were razors and figurines. Bronze razors were common in the western territories such as Carthage and commonly figured in burial goods. It is likely that the razor was buried with the owner as a deeply personal item as it would have been used on a regular basis. Razors were considered a male item, while mirrors and combs made of bronze were more feminine. Figurines served as votive offerings for religious ceremonies and typically depicted goddesses in Egyptian dress with their hand outstretched as a gesture of welcome or offering.[22]

Ivory and Stone Sculptures

The Phoenicians were one of the first cultures from the Levant to acquire ivory in sufficient numbers to produce artwork. Ivory formed an integral part of the artwork in the ancient world, and the Phoenicians rapidly increased the demand for it by crafting exquisite sculptures and images that were sold throughout the Near East and Africa. The ivory came from city-states and colonies in North Africa, where there was an adequate elephant population to supply the material. Phoenician ivory objects have been discovered throughout the Levantine coast and in Iraq, Italy, Greece, and on numerous Mediterranean islands.

---

[22] There continues to be a debate about whether or not these figurines are male or female, with the majority of archaeologists believing the statues are feminine in nature.

Ivory sculptures and artifacts can be divided between the large and the small. The majority of discovered large objects hail from 900 to 800 BCE and mainly include furniture panels for tables, beds, chairs, footstools, and even thrones. These panels were designed to form decorative motifs when properly installed and appeared in items with gold filigree, colorful glass paste, and even precious and semiprecious gems.

Smaller objects are by far more numerous. Ivory was a popular material for toiletries such as combs and mirrors. Another frequently found item is the ivory box, which was small enough to potentially hold someone's jewelry and ornaments. Some historians believe these smaller pieces were made from the leftovers produced by the creation of larger objects. This assumption is based on the fact that elephant tusks were transported from northern Syria and were easier to work and shape when left in one piece. The long furniture panels show evidence of being carved from one piece as well.

Stone sculpture did not enjoy the success that many other mediums had. Although stone was accessible in the coastal city-states and colonies, artisans did not focus on this substance. The only times stone appeared were in wall reliefs and sarcophagi, large pieces that took advantage of preexisting stones that required little shaping. Instead, artisans worked through carving and did not develop many standalone stone sculptures or statues. Manufacturers produced stone caskets with masculine or feminine outlines on the top to indicate the occupant, and headstones were also developed with this material.

The Stone Sarcophagus of King Ahiram of Byblos, c. 1000s BCE

Textiles

Although few textiles survived the test of time, the Phoenicians had a reputation for creating some of the finest and most richly dyed fabrics using local cotton, wool, and flax. These were well woven and used the signature murex purple dye that the civilization was renowned for. Textiles were transported by ship throughout the Mediterranean and even made an appearance in modern Abrahamic religious texts. Unfortunately, not a shred of that fabric is preserved today.

Conclusion – The Legacy of the Phoenicians

Although the sands of time took much of the history of the Phoenicians, this civilization's legacy lives on through the effects of its culture, education, and extensive trade networks. One of the most significant was the trend of alphabets being used throughout the Mediterranean to improve the literacy of not only hierarchical priests but also merchants, traders, and influential craftsmen and women. They also reopened the trade routes of the Eastern Mediterranean that had fallen during the Bronze Age Collapse, thus connecting the Greeks, Romans, Anatolians, and the Carthaginians to the Egyptian and Mesopotamian civilizations. Such an act would eventually lead to the "Orientalizing" of Greek art, or the implementation of more Eastern elements in murals and sculptures.

When it comes to politics, the Phoenicians were one of the first developers of an oligarchic social structure with roots in democracy. This was exemplified by the ability of the city-states to have influential merchants and traders who were not necessarily royals or nobles but who were still able to exert their will on traditionally hierarchical structures. Some historians believe the Phoenicians would inspire the Greek Athenian revolution and the development of a Greek constitutional government. Continuing the influence on Greece, many historians believe that Zeno of Citium, the founder of the famous school of philosophy known as Stoicism, was Phoenician.

Of course, there were other avenues of significance, especially related to the development of military and naval technology and the advancements that were copied by or passed down to the Greeks, Romans, and Etruscans. Although the Phoenicians won few great military victories, they demonstrated the power of currency by dominating their neighbors with financial strangleholds. It could be said that they proved how the pen might be mightier than the sword, but the coin outweighs them all.

While these may seem insignificant to the average individual living in contemporary society, the Phoenicians helped establish elements of both Western and Eastern cultures by reestablishing contact between civilizations following the Bronze Age Collapse. If contact had been allowed to fade, modern humans would have lost thousands of years of international trade and culture sharing, meaning the rich Mediterranean history of symbolism and exchange might not have ever occurred or would have happened in a different way entirely. How many people enjoy advancements like Judaism and Christianity in the West, and elements of modern warfare like ranged weapons in the East? What about purple clothes? Mathematics? Democratic civilization?

Without the Phoenicians to bridge the gap between the East and West, who knows when civilizations would have united once more to share culture and scientific developments. While the Mediterranean may have warred, trade fostered deep connections and ensured advancements could be shared throughout the Asian, European, and African continents.

Read more Captivating History Books about Ancient History

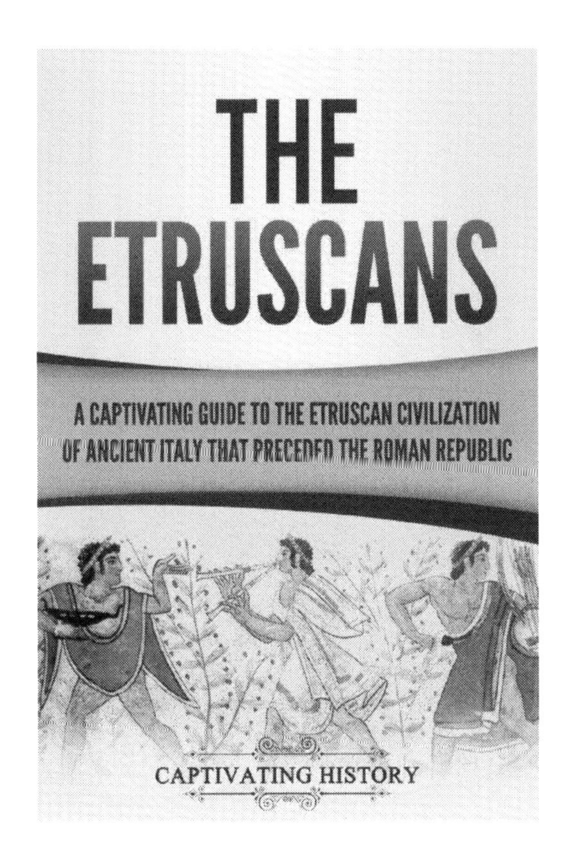
THE
ETRUSCANS
A CAPTIVATING GUIDE TO THE ETRUSCAN CIVILIZATION
OF ANCIENT ITALY THAT PRECEDED THE ROMAN REPUBLIC
CAPTIVATING HISTORY

Bibliography

Barnett, Richard D. "Phoenicia and the Ivory Trade." *Archaeology* 9, no. 2 (1956): 87-97.

Bikai, Patricia M. "The Phoenicians: A Bibliography." *Bulletin of the American Schools of Oriental Research*, no. 279 (1990): 65-66.

Chaney, William R. and Basbous, Malek. "The Cedars of Lebanon: Witnesses of History." *Economic Botany* 32, no. 2 (1978): 118-123.

Elayi, Josette. *A monetary and political history of the Phoenician city of Byblos in the fifth and fourth centuries BCE.* Winona Lake: Eisenbrauns, 2014.

Elayi, Josette. *The History of Phoenicia.* Lockwood Press, 2018.

Ercolani, Andrea and Xella, Paolo. *Encyclopedic Dictionary of Phoenician culture.* Peeters Publishing, 2018.

Martin, Rebecca S. *The art of contact: comparative approaches to Greek and Phoenician art.* Philadelphia: University of Pennsylvania Press, 2017.

Moreno Garcia, Juan Carlos. *Dynamics of production in the Ancient Near East: 1300-500 BC.* Philadelphia: Oxbow Books, 2016.

Peckham, J. Brian. *Phoenicia: Episodes and Anecdotes from the Ancient Mediterranean.* Eisenbrauns Publishing, 2014.

Sherratt, Susan. "Greeks and Phoenicians: Perception of Trade and Traders in the Early First Millennium BC." In *Social Archaeologies of Trade and Exchange: Exploring Relationships Among People, Places, and Things* by Alexander A. Bauer, Anna S. Agbe-Davies, and Robert W. Preucel, p. 119-142. Walnut Creek: Left Coast Press, 2010.

Woolmer, Mark. *A Short History of the Phoenicians.* New York: I. B. Tauris, 2017.

Woolmer, Mark. *Ancient Phoenicia: An Introduction.* London: Bristol Classic Press, 2011.

Made in the USA
Columbia, SC
17 June 2021